Regency

Coloring Book

Aryla Publishing 2021

978-1-912675-46-3

www.arylapublishing.com

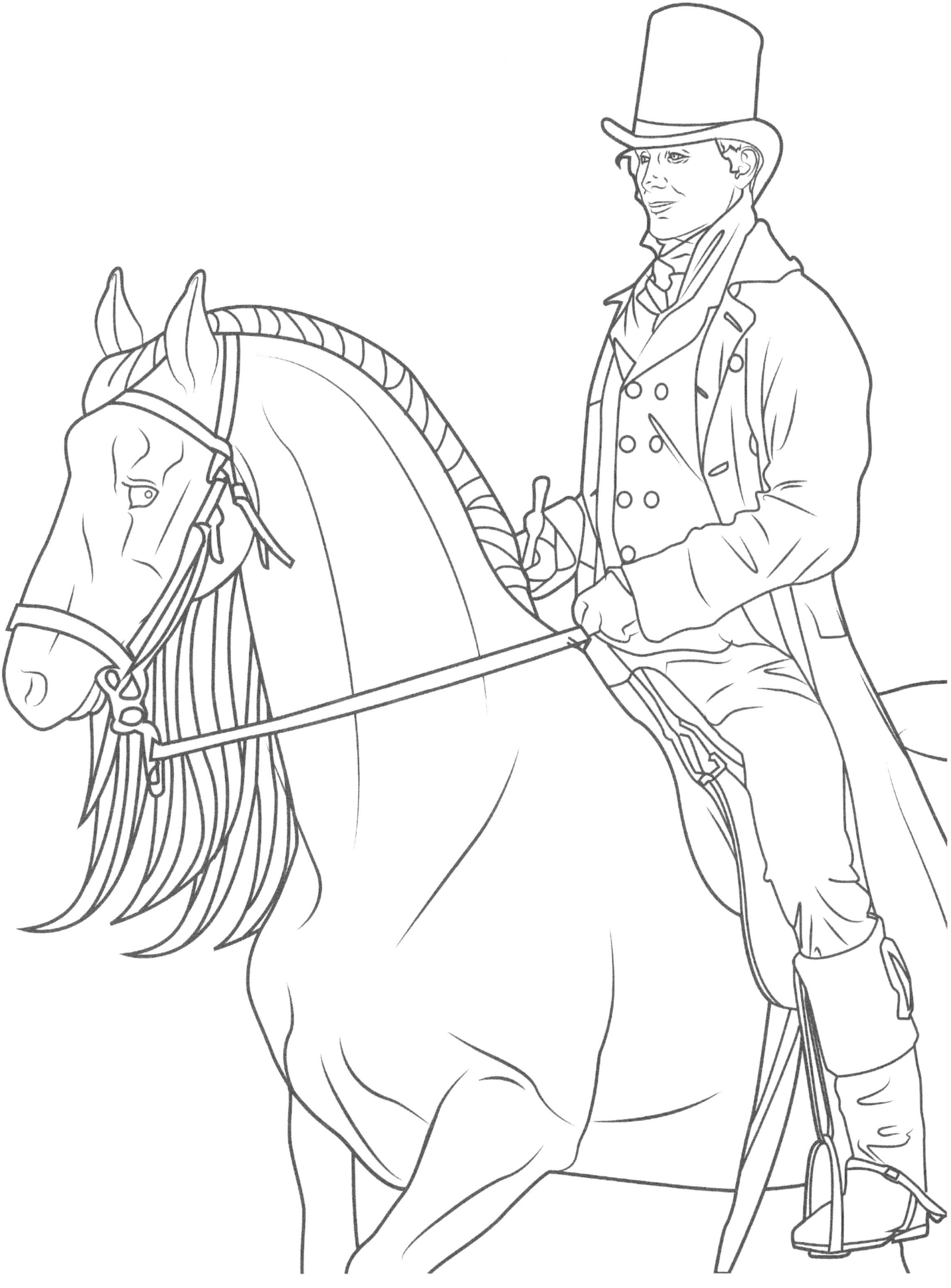

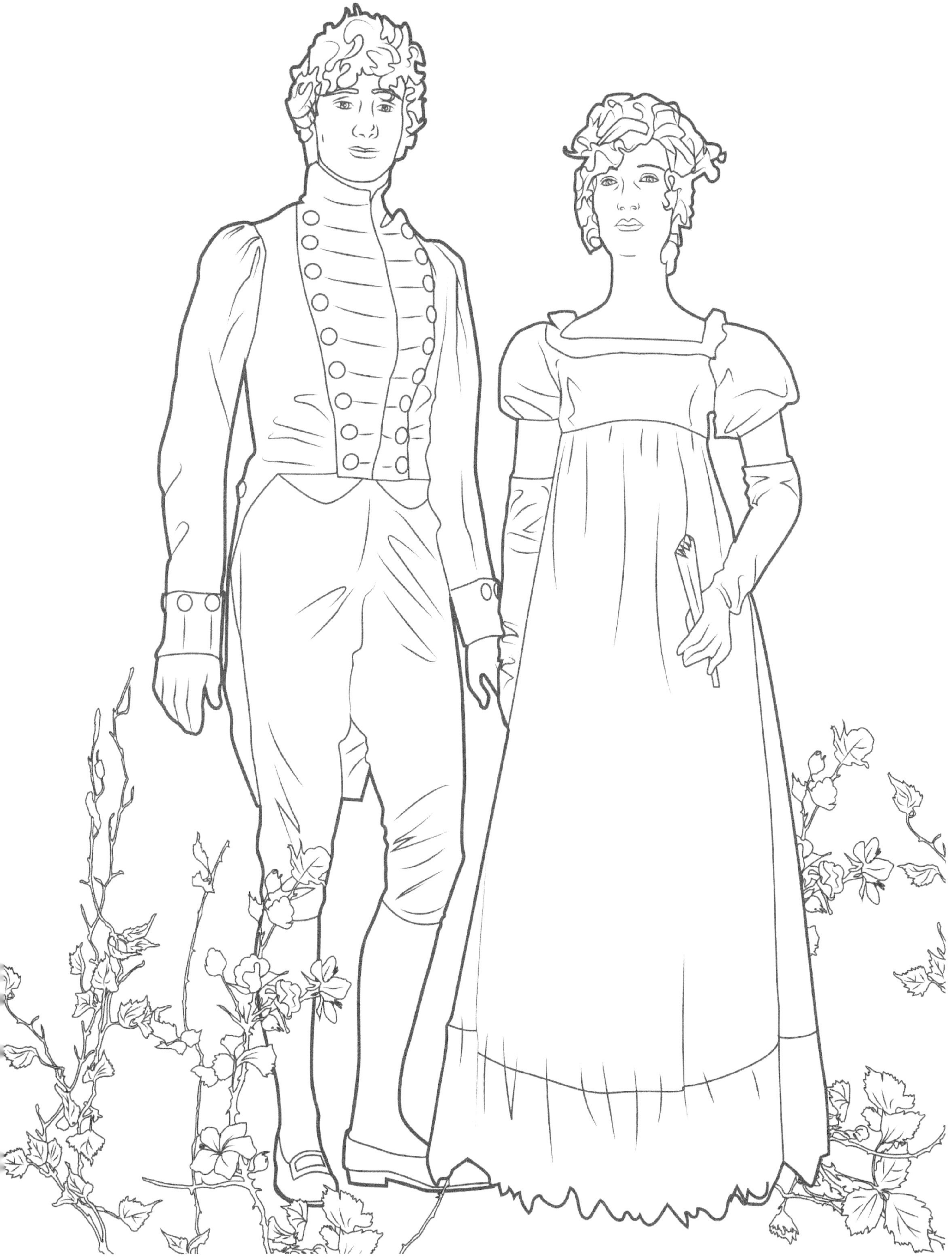

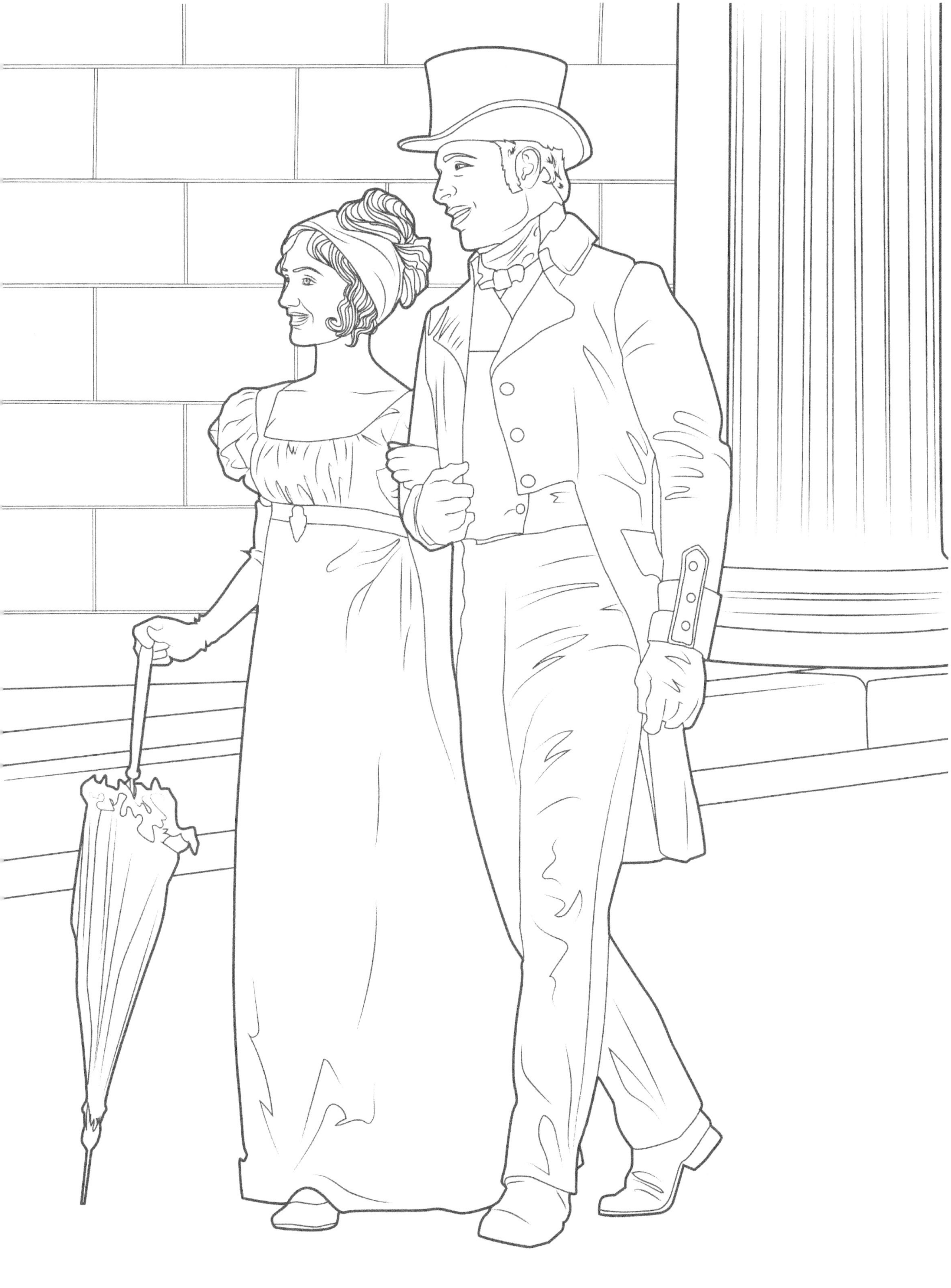

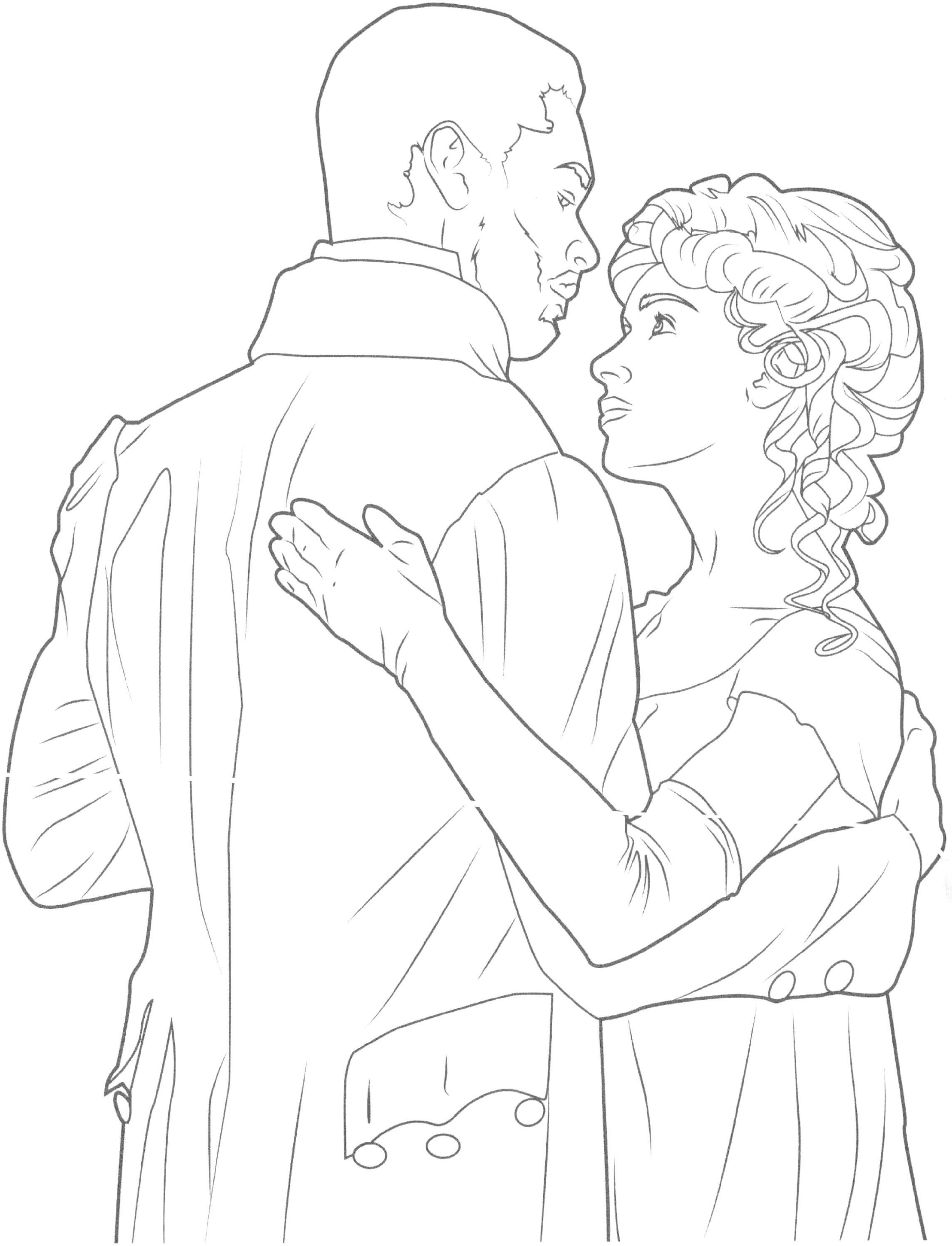

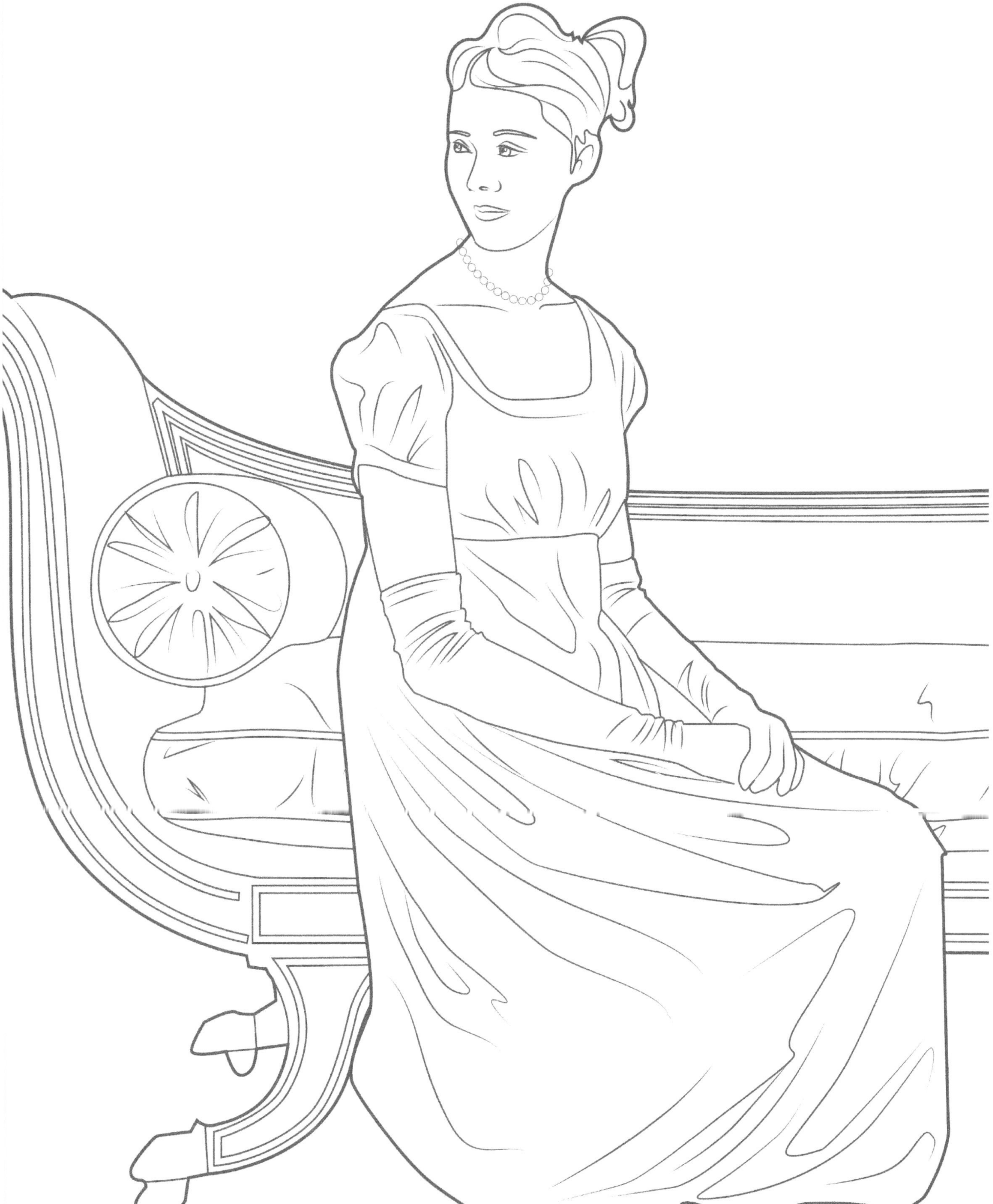

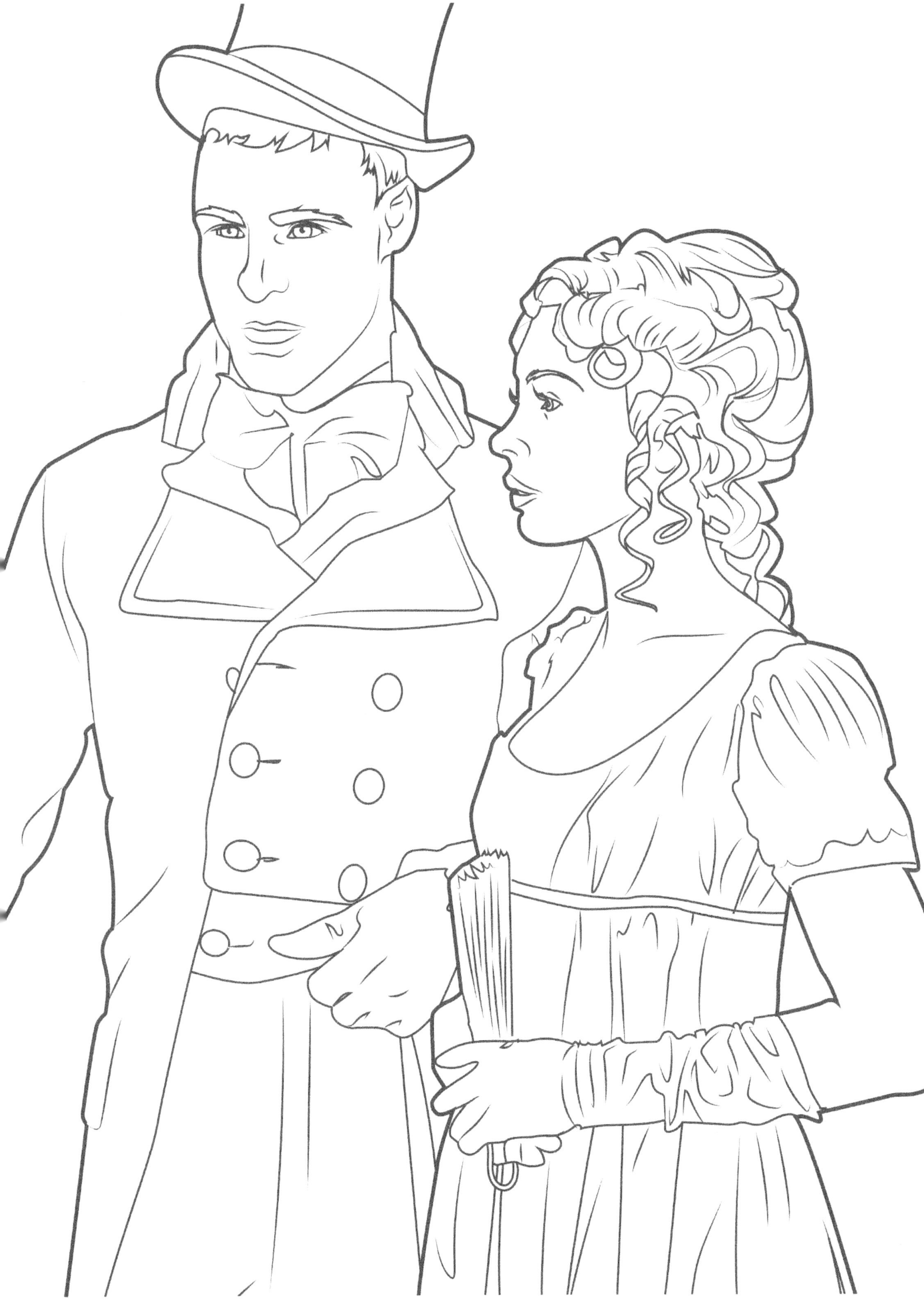

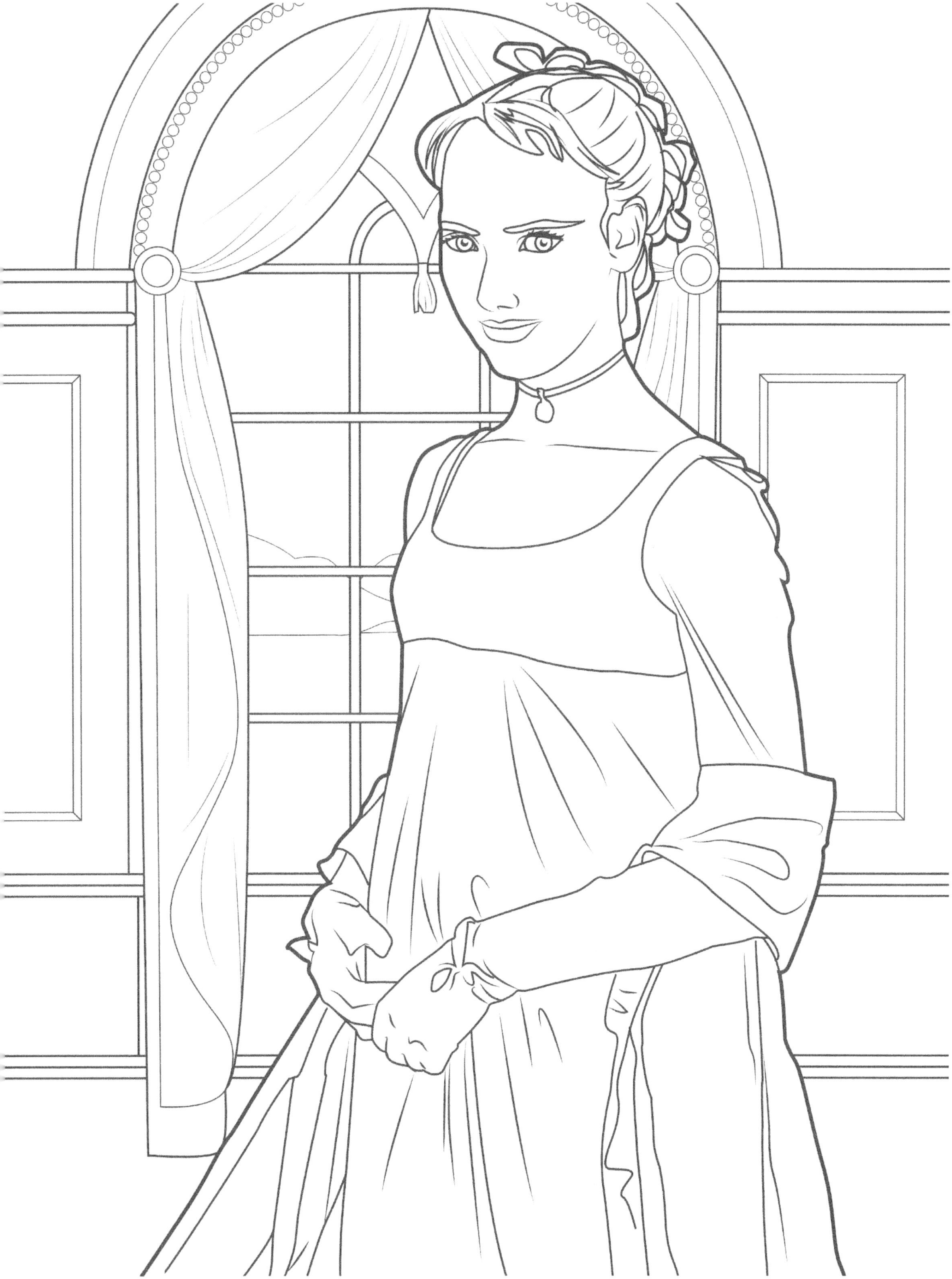

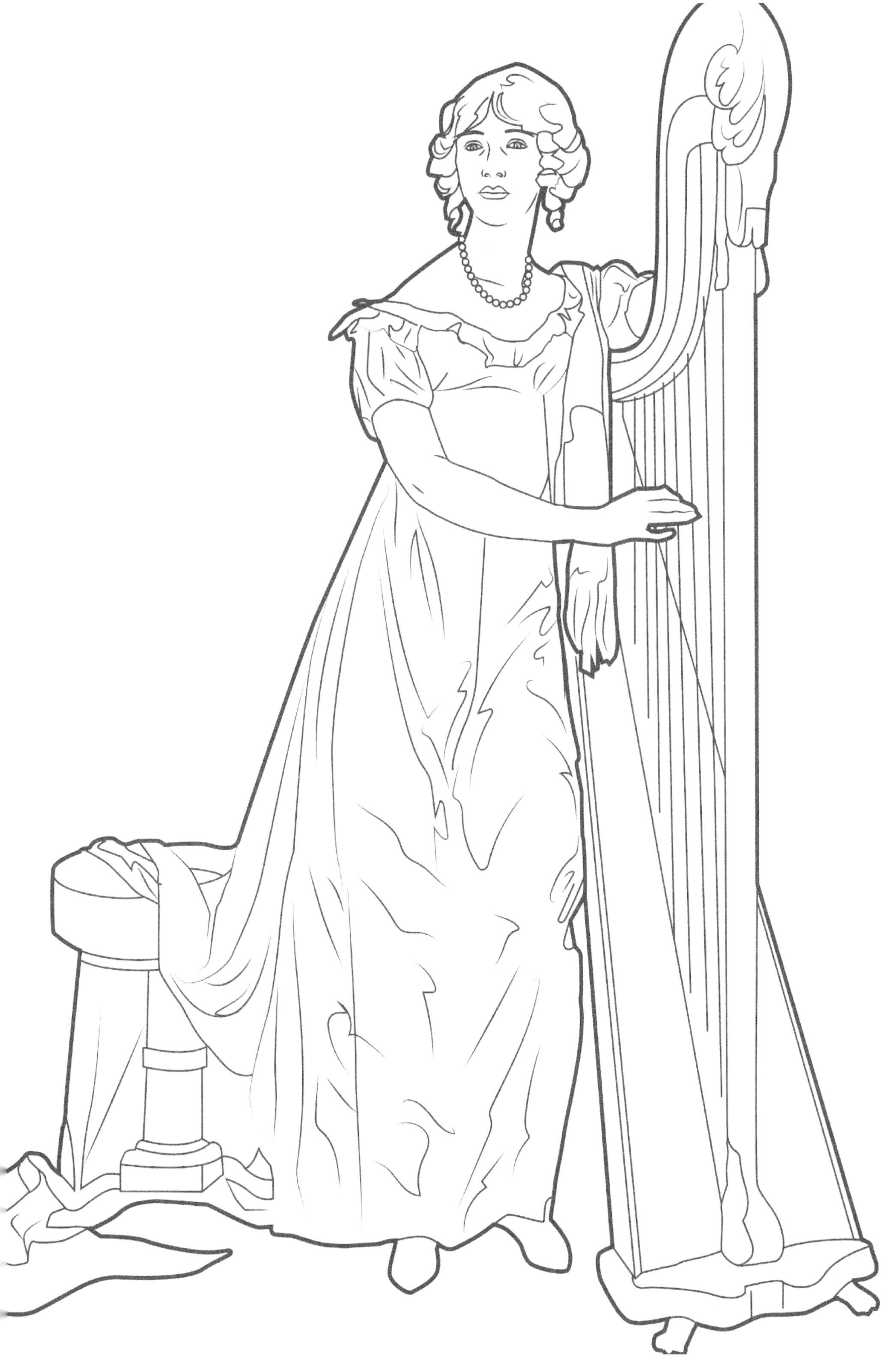

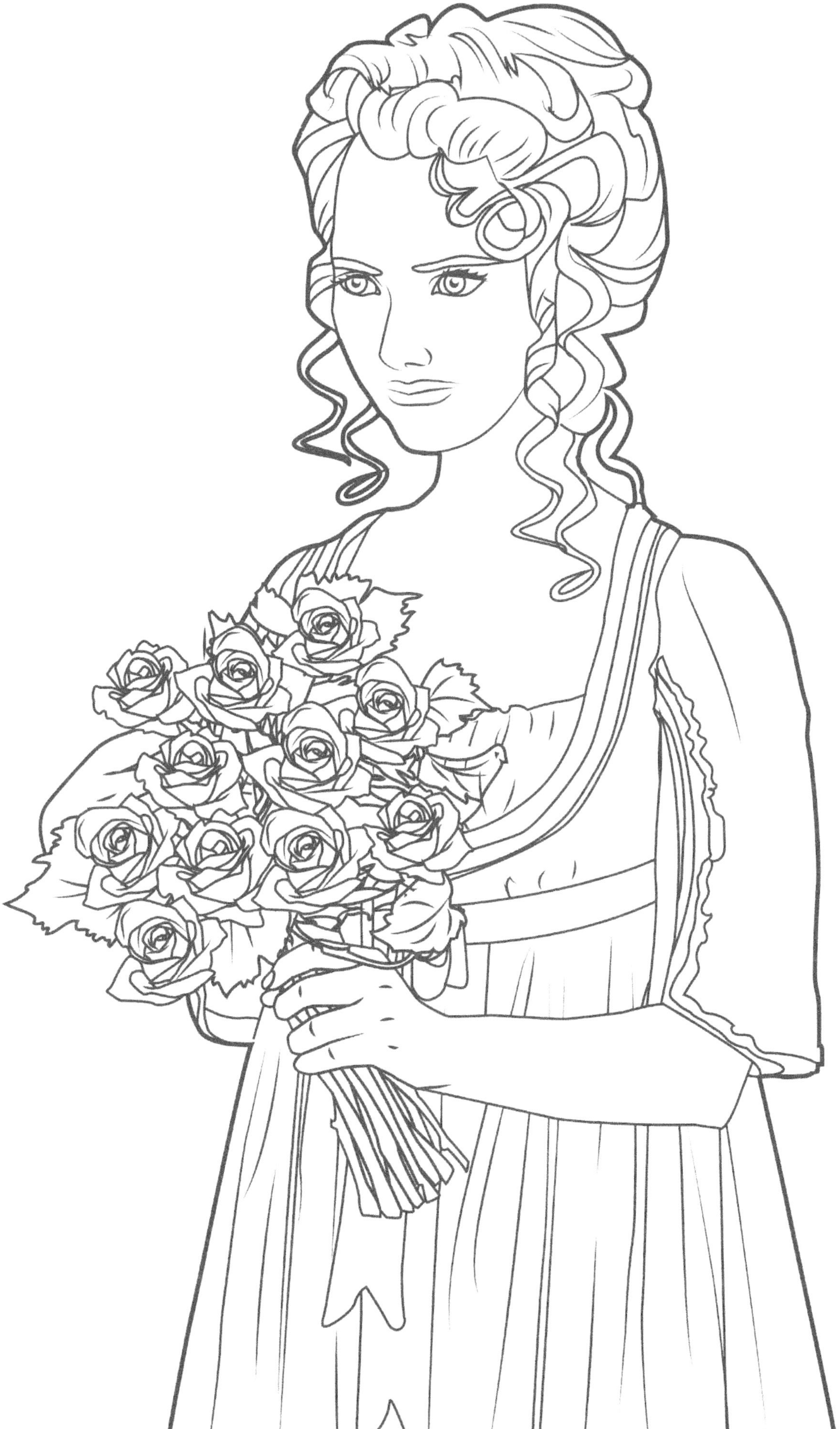

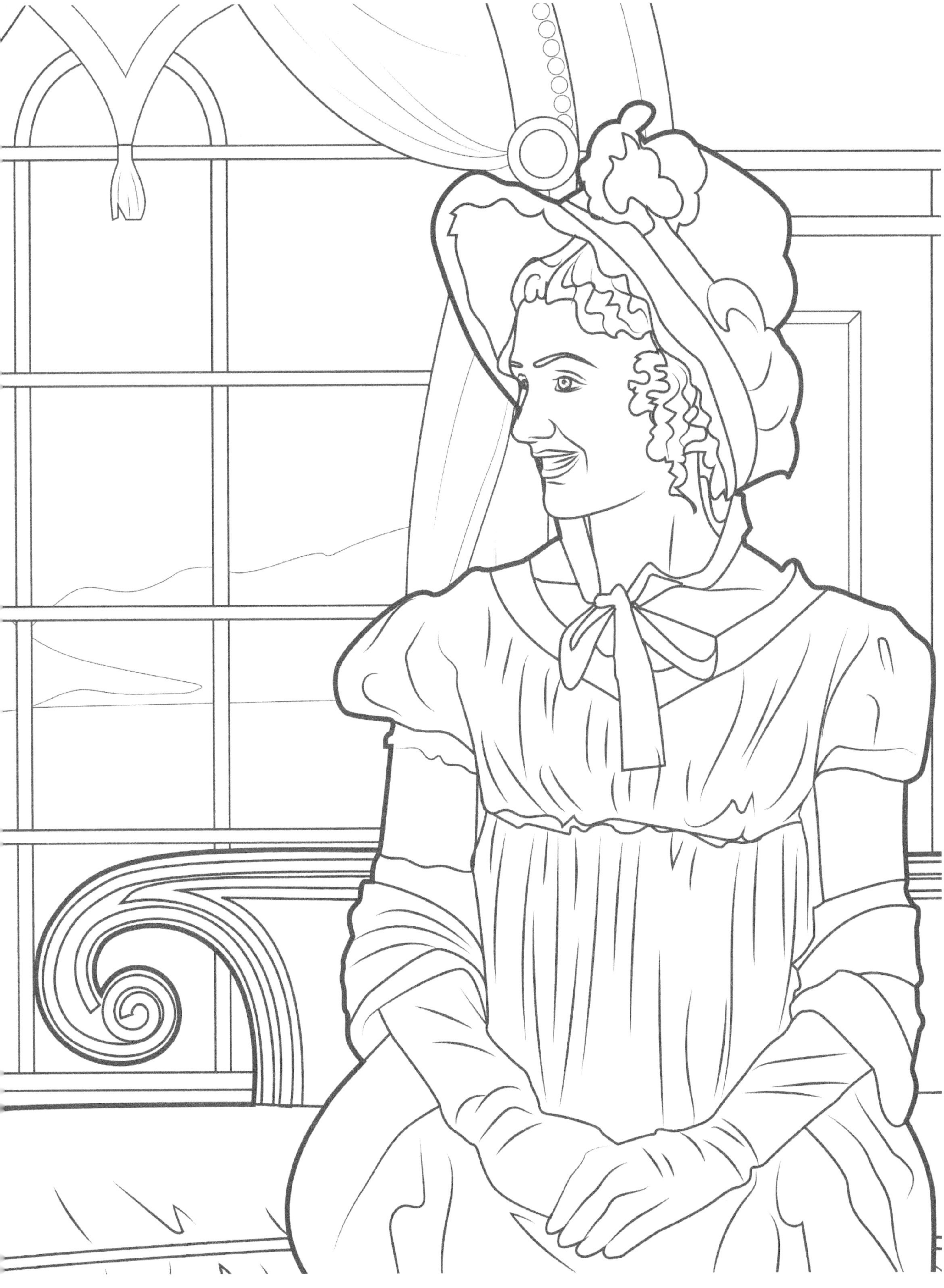

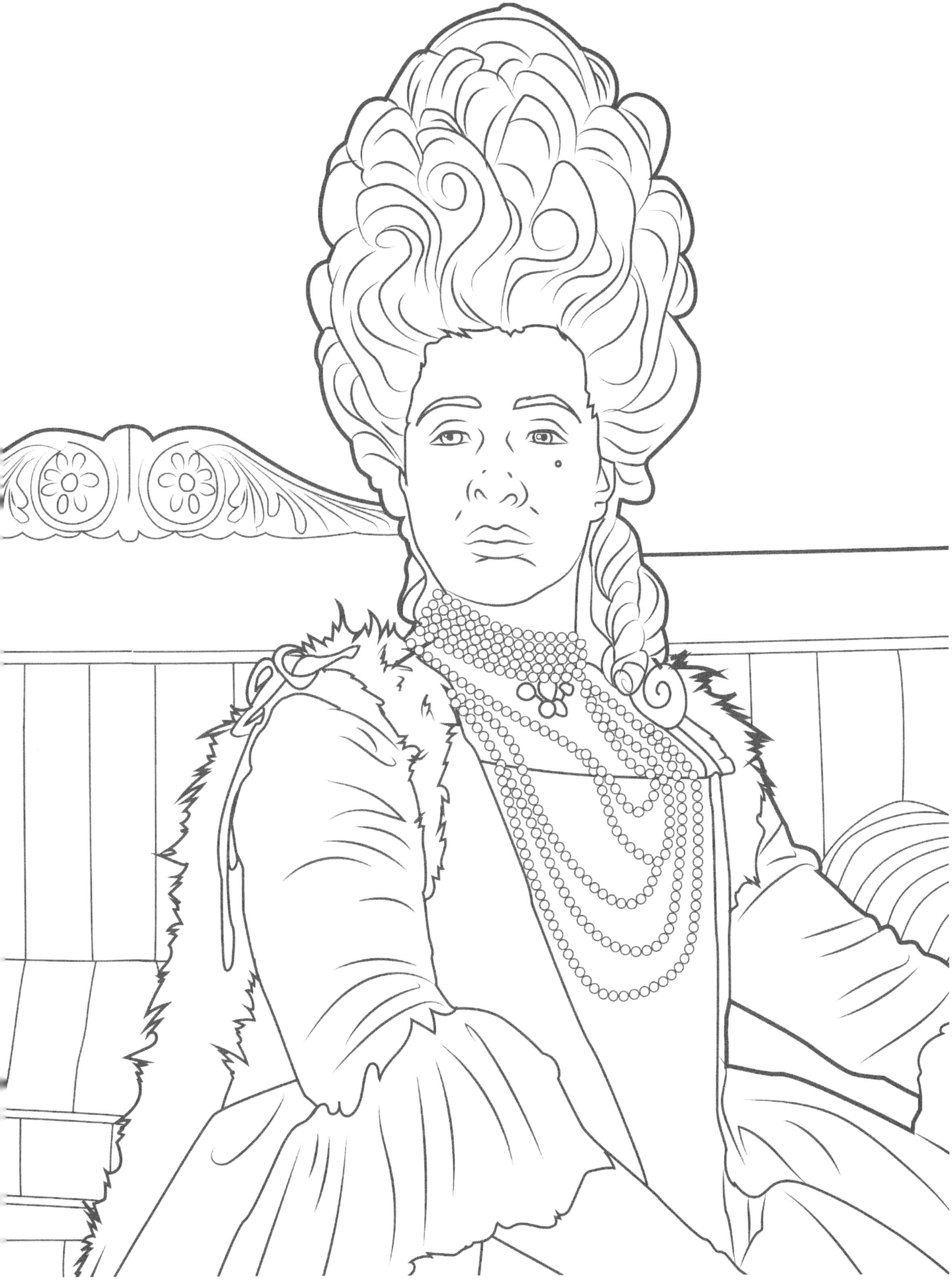

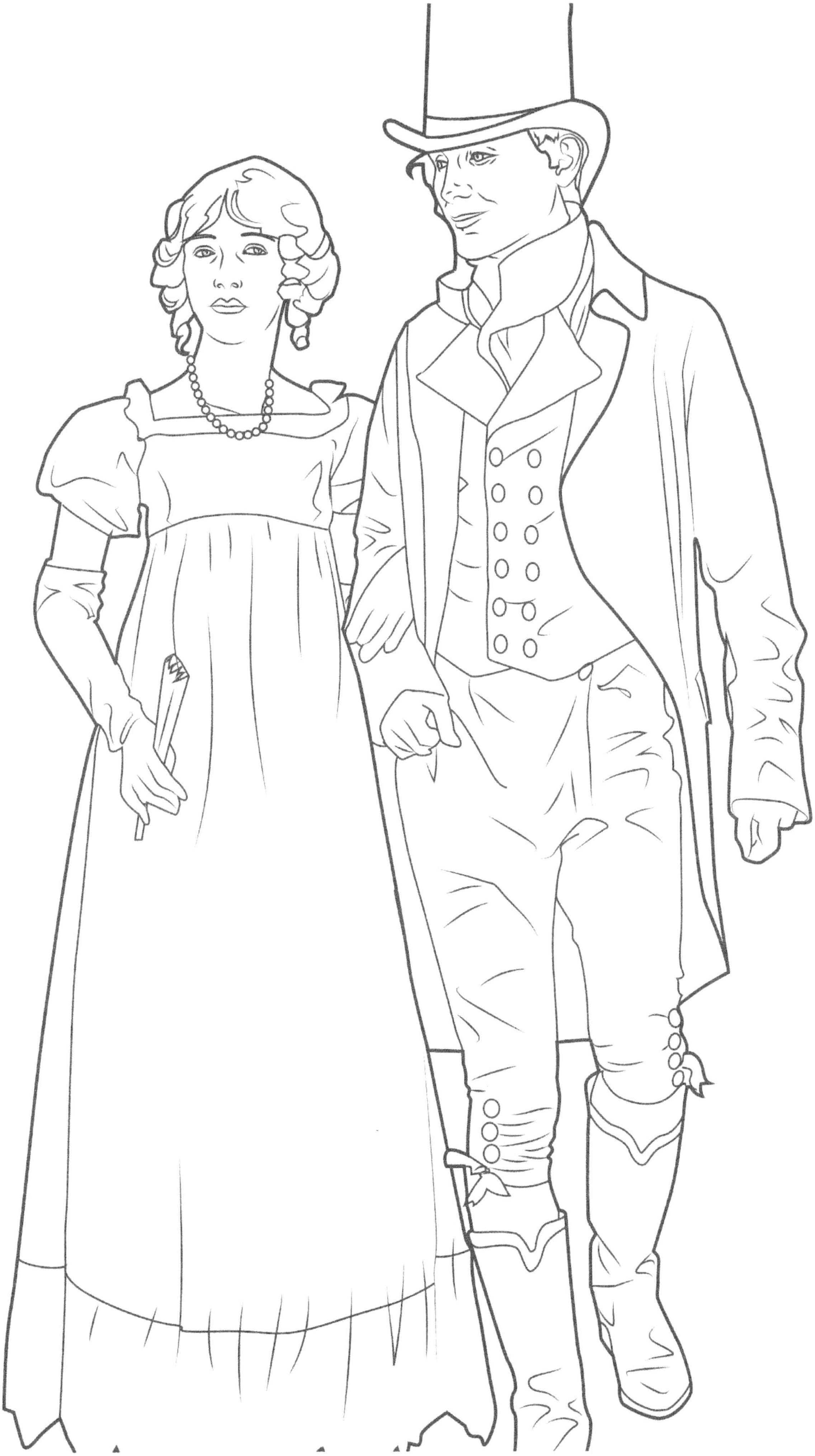

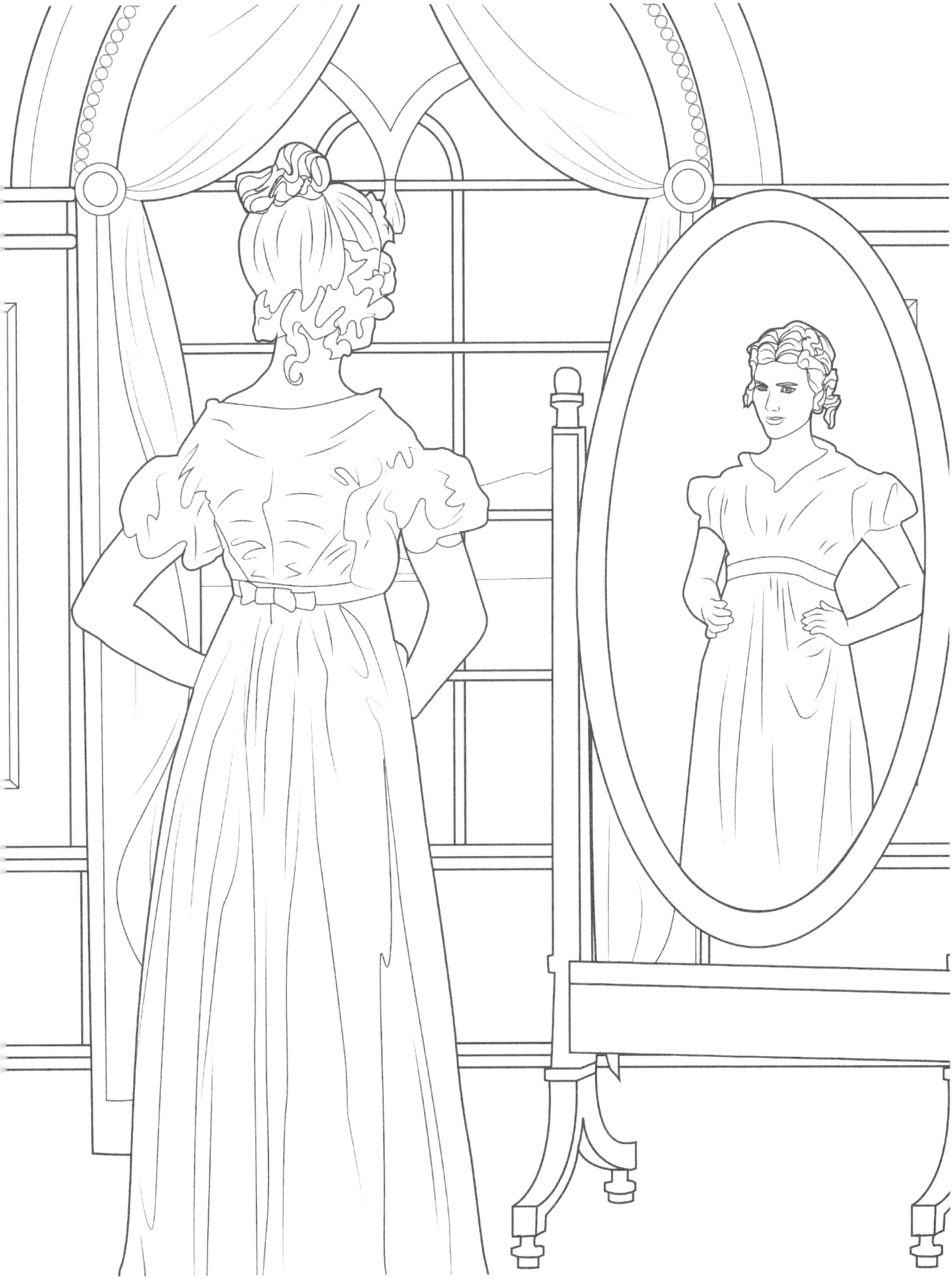

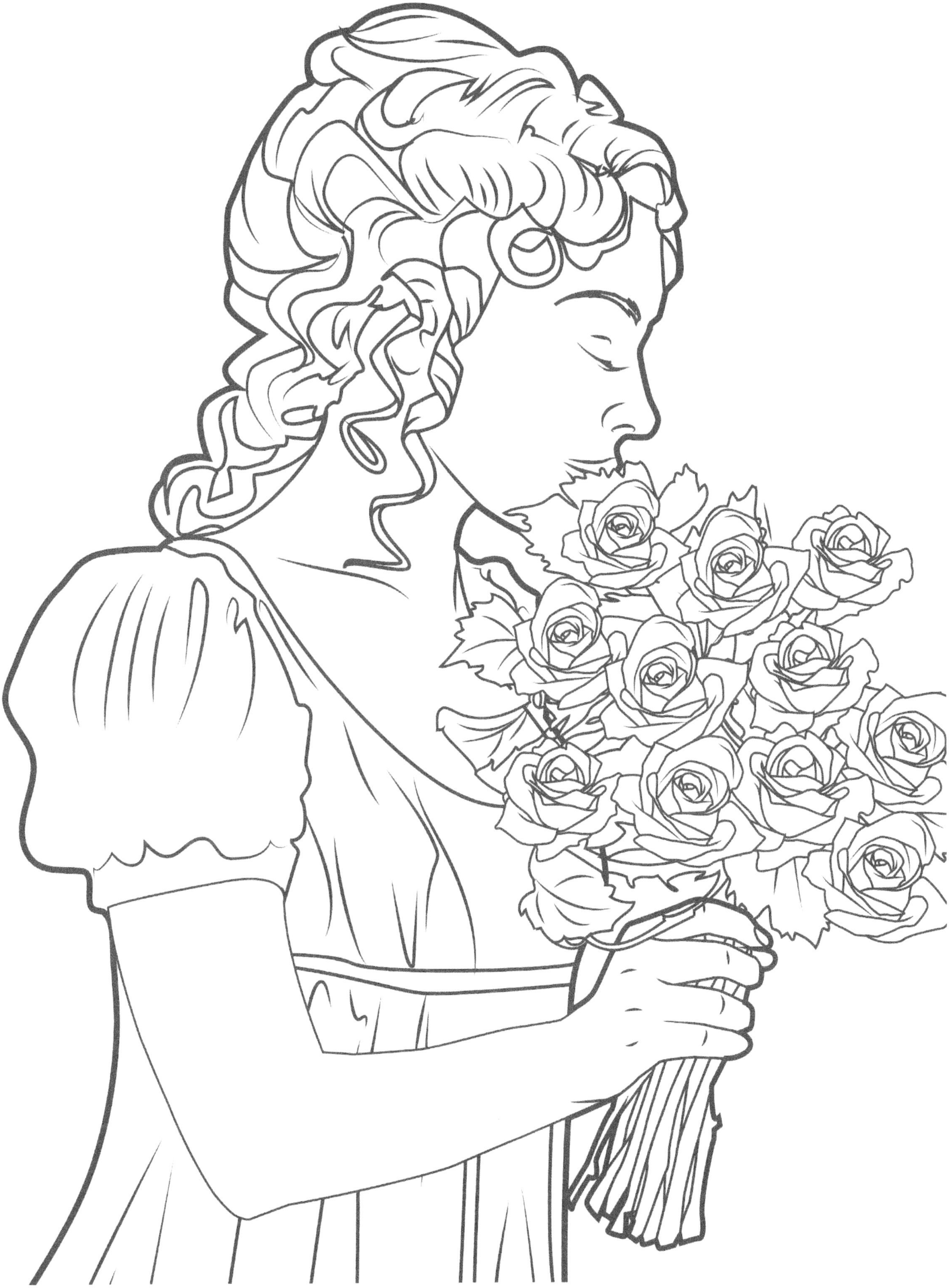

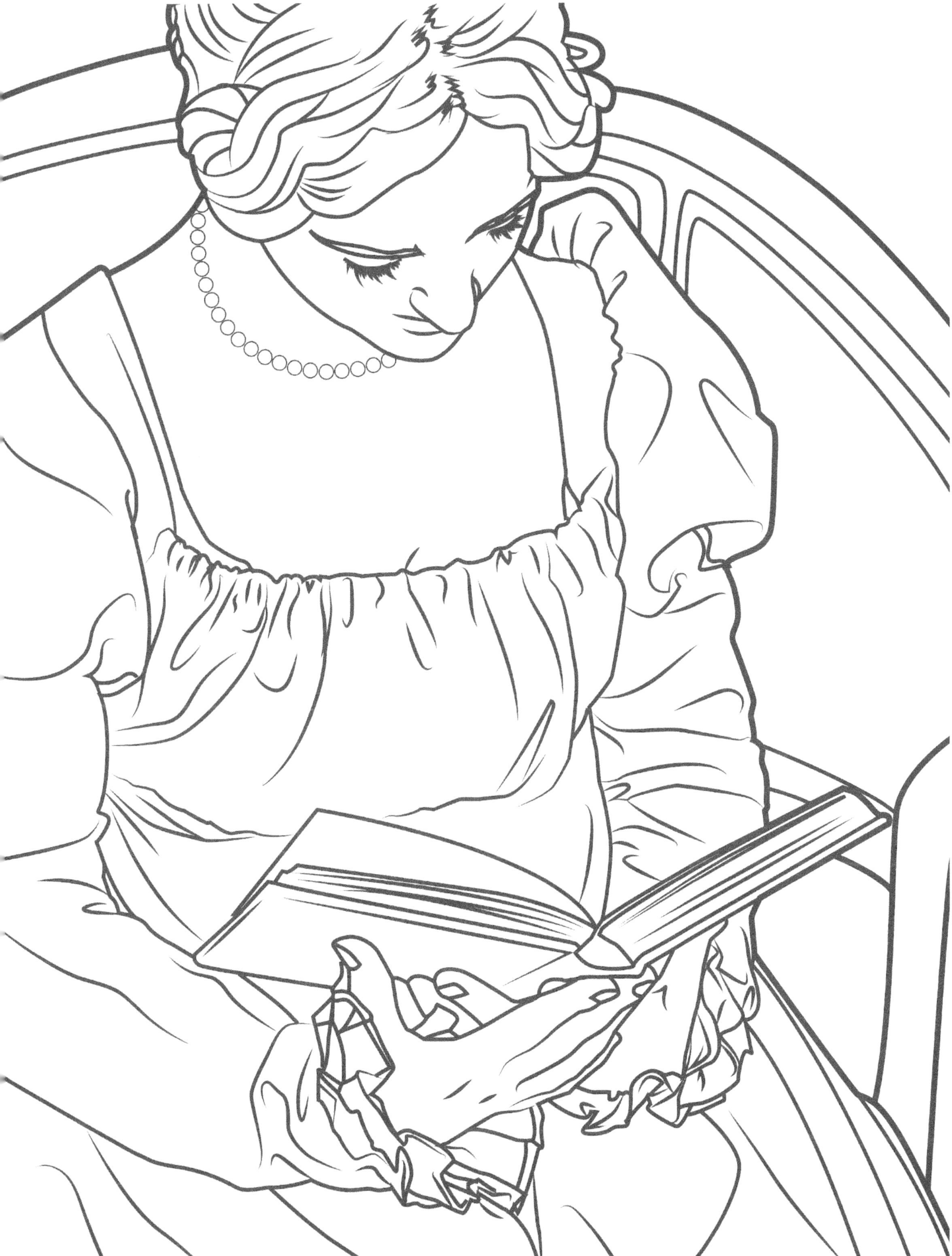

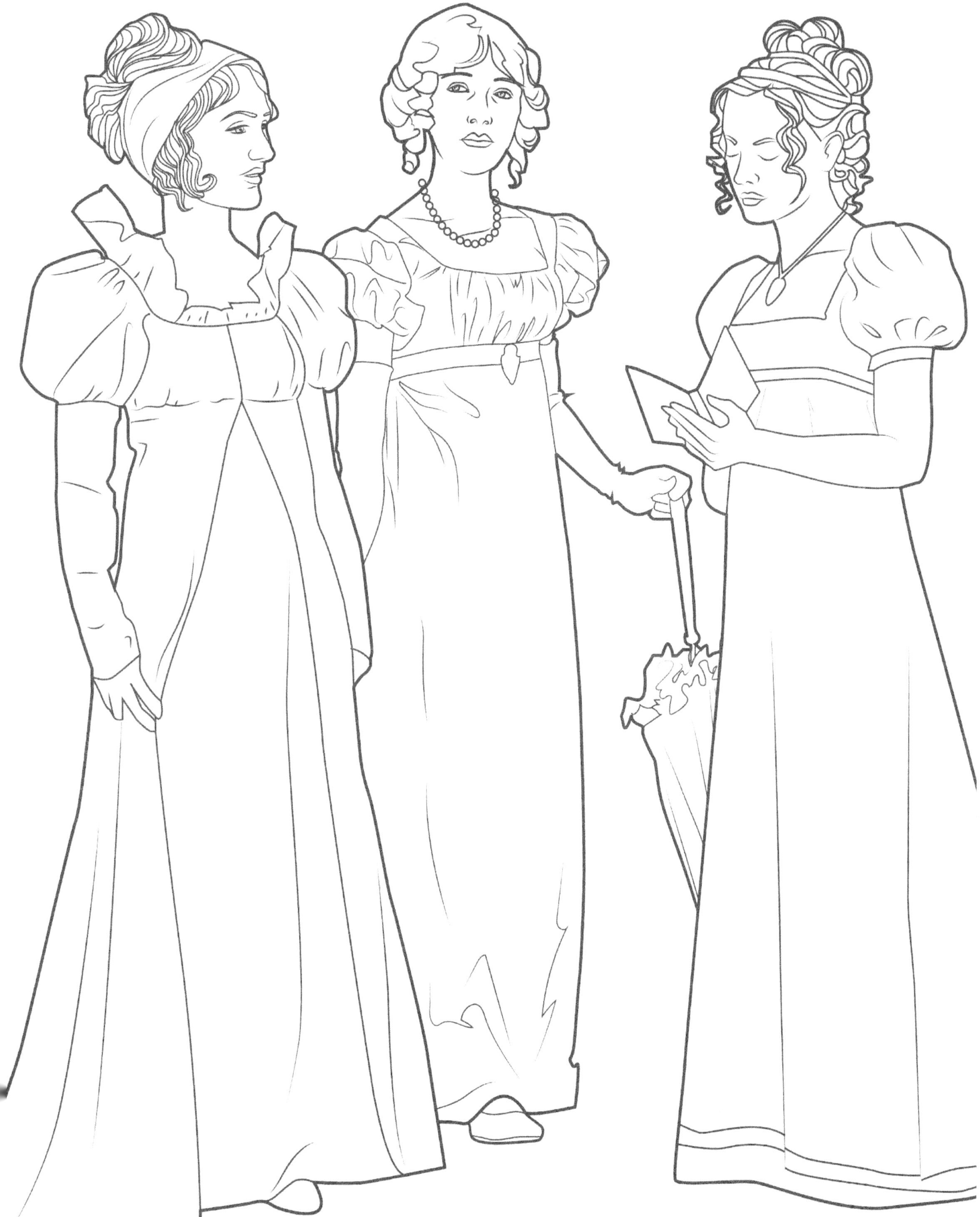

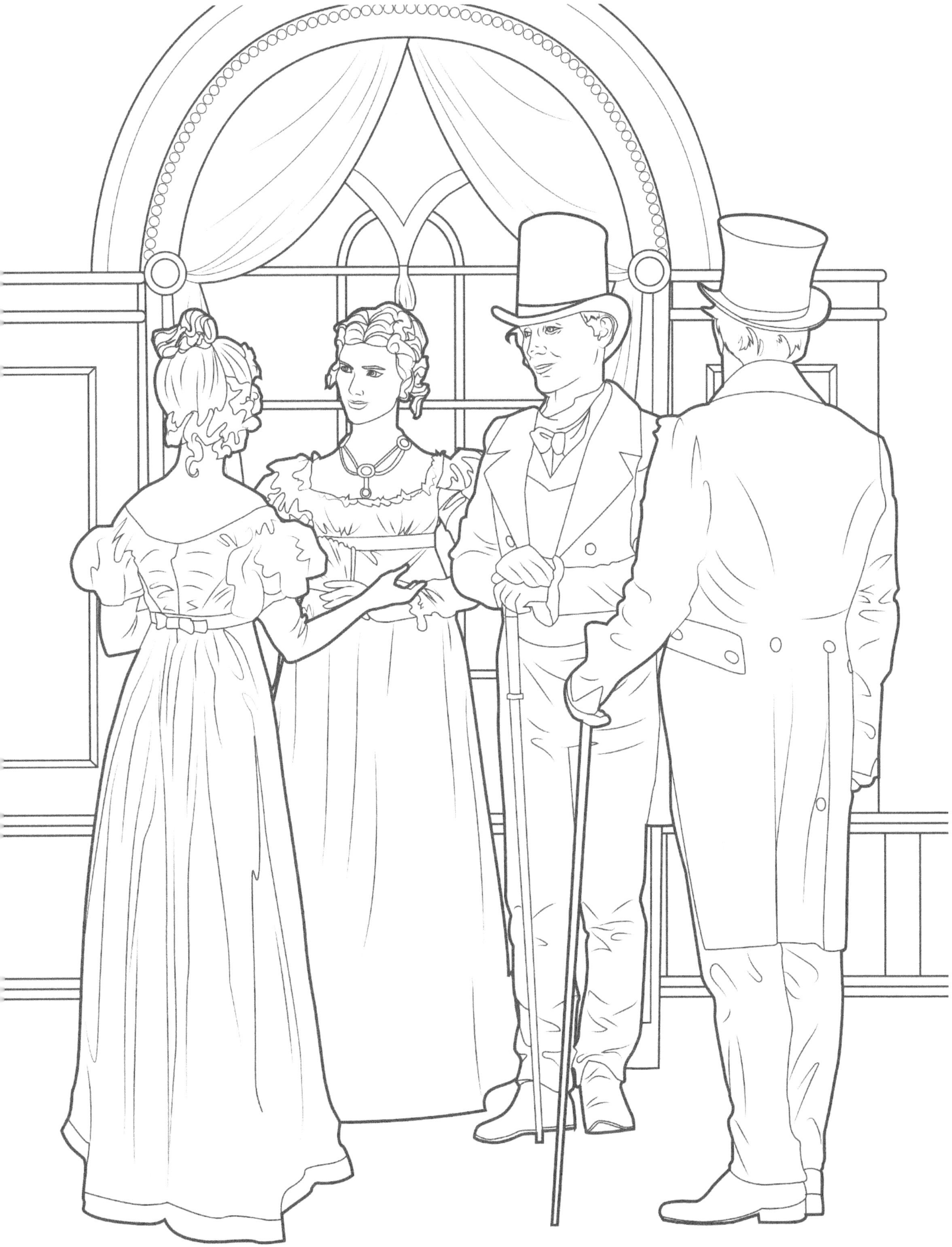

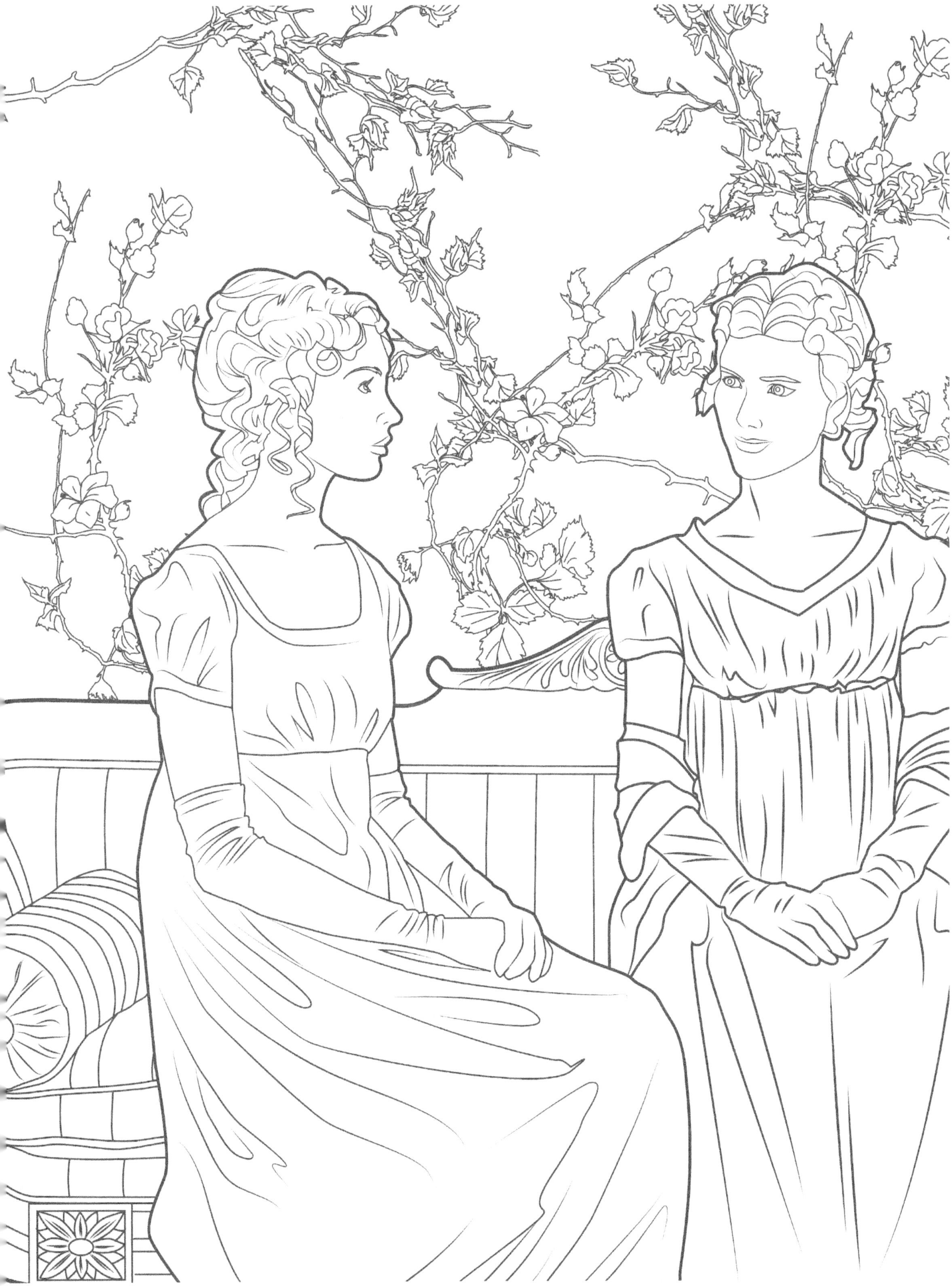

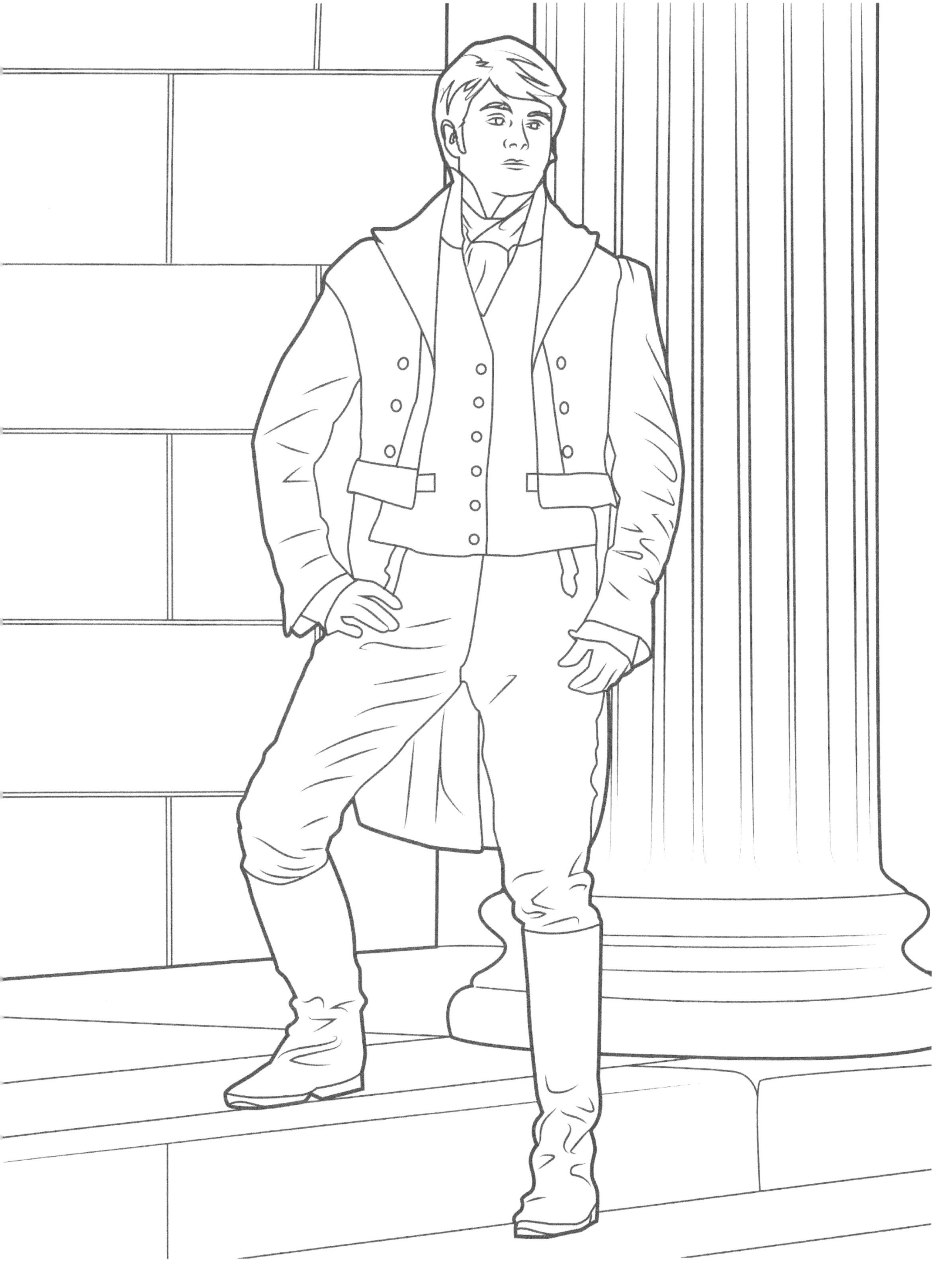

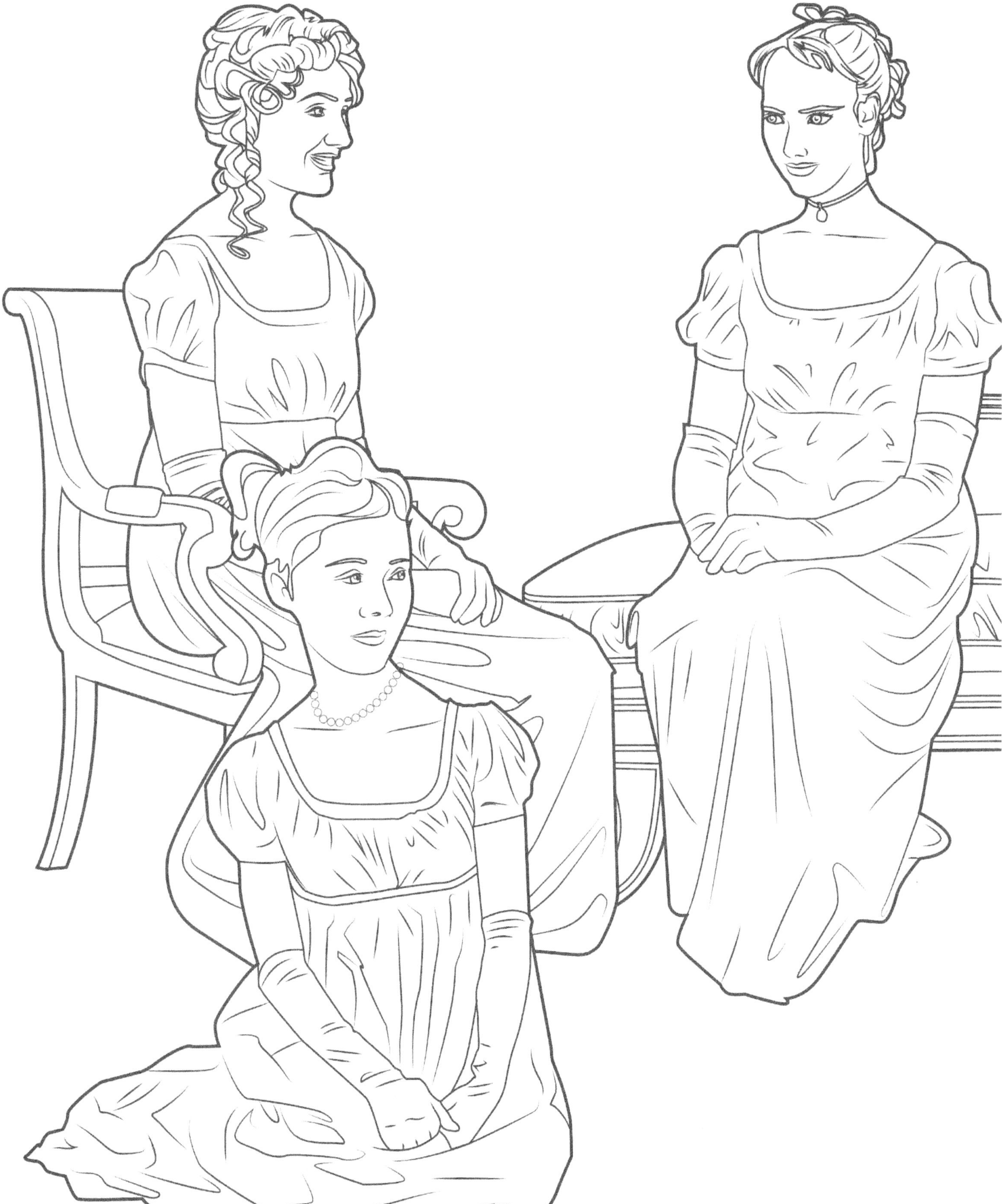

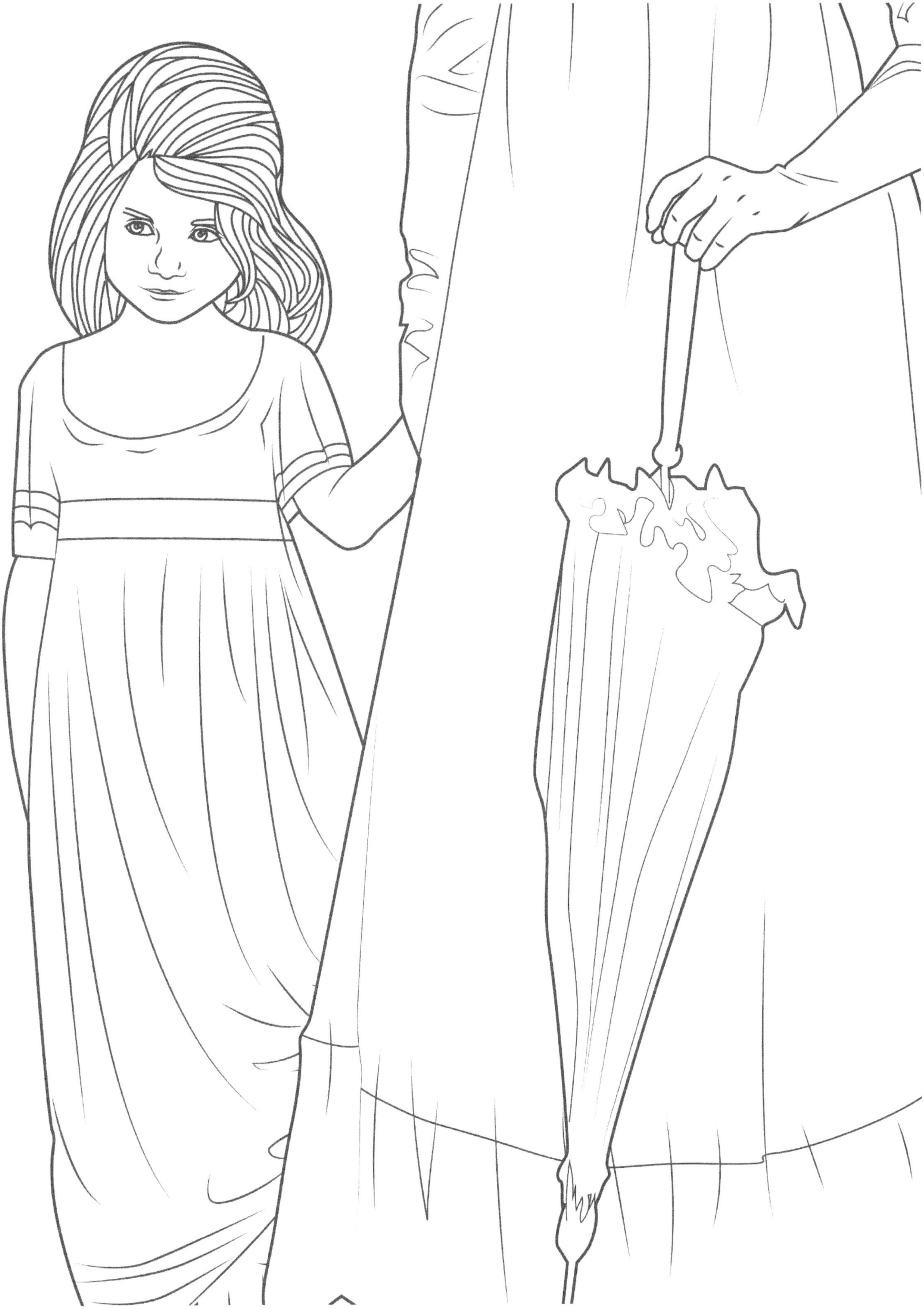

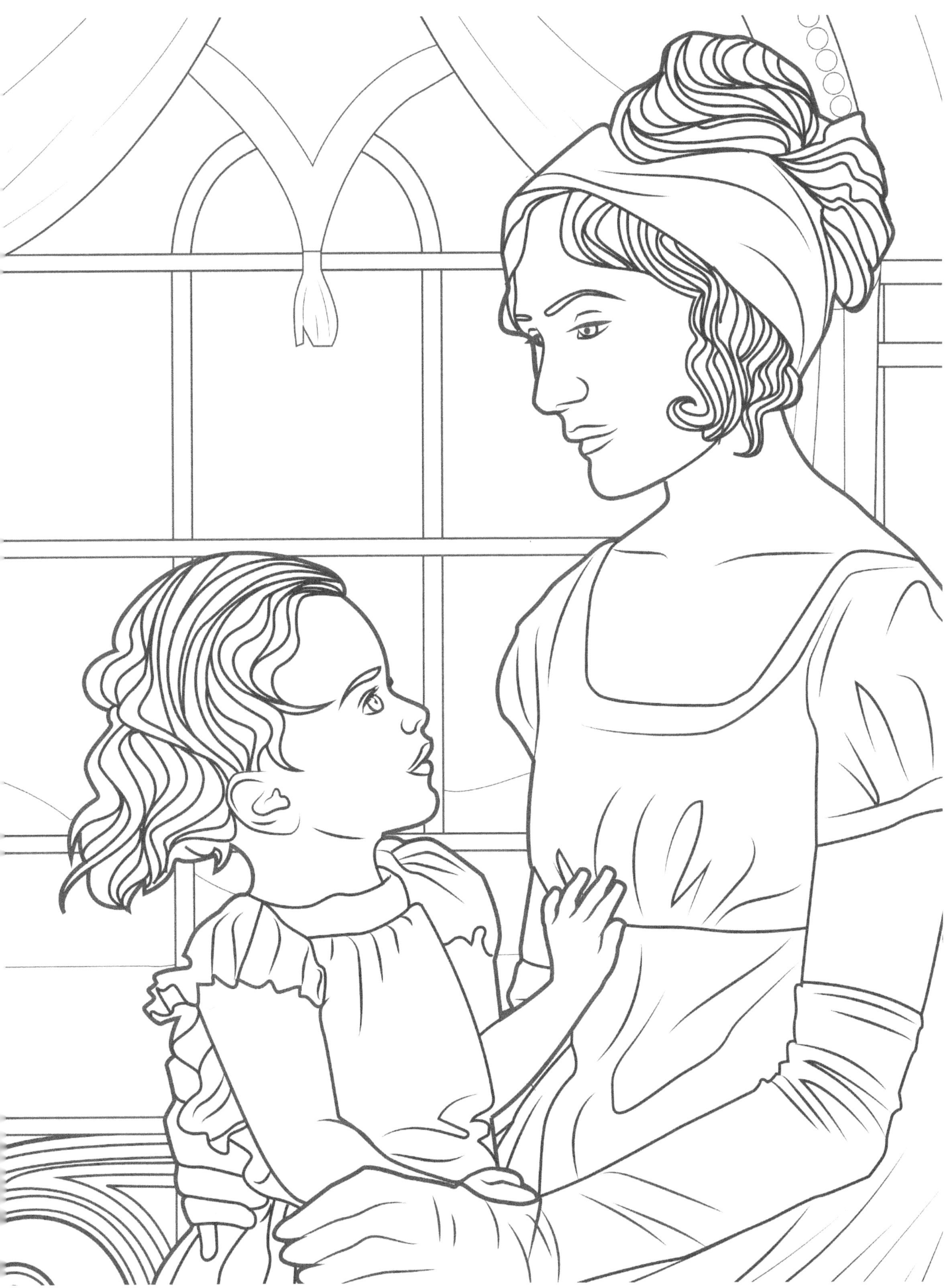

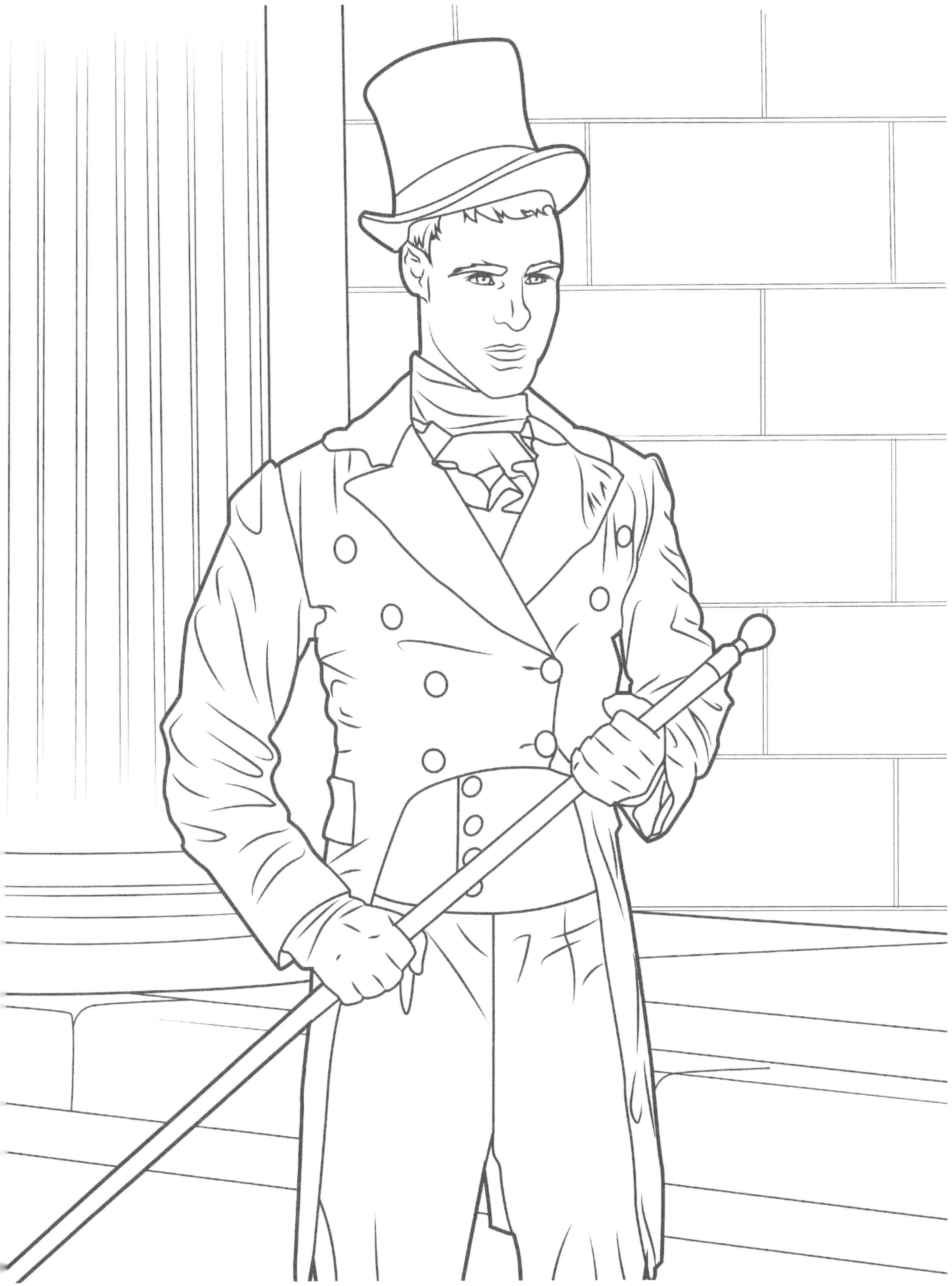

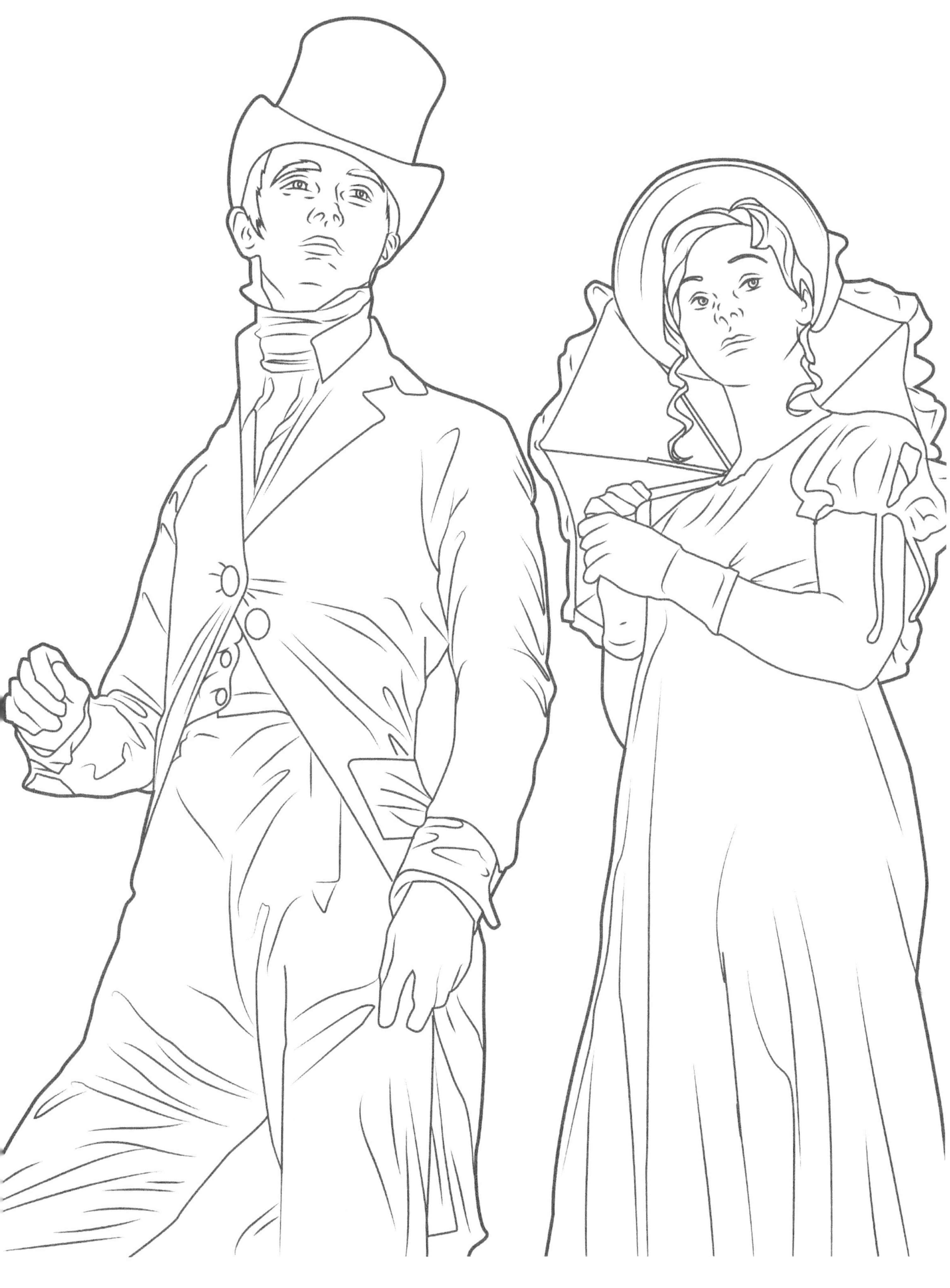

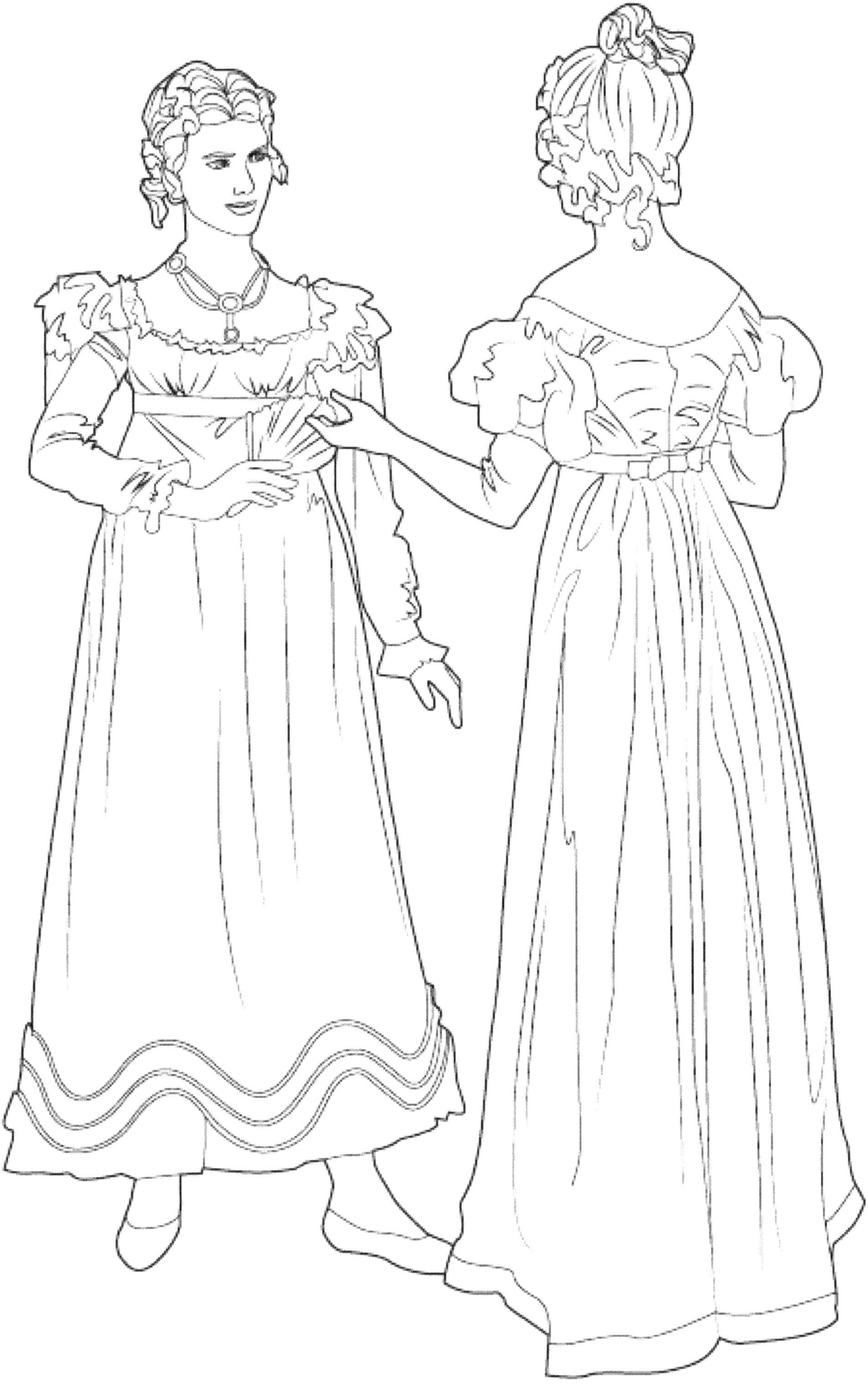

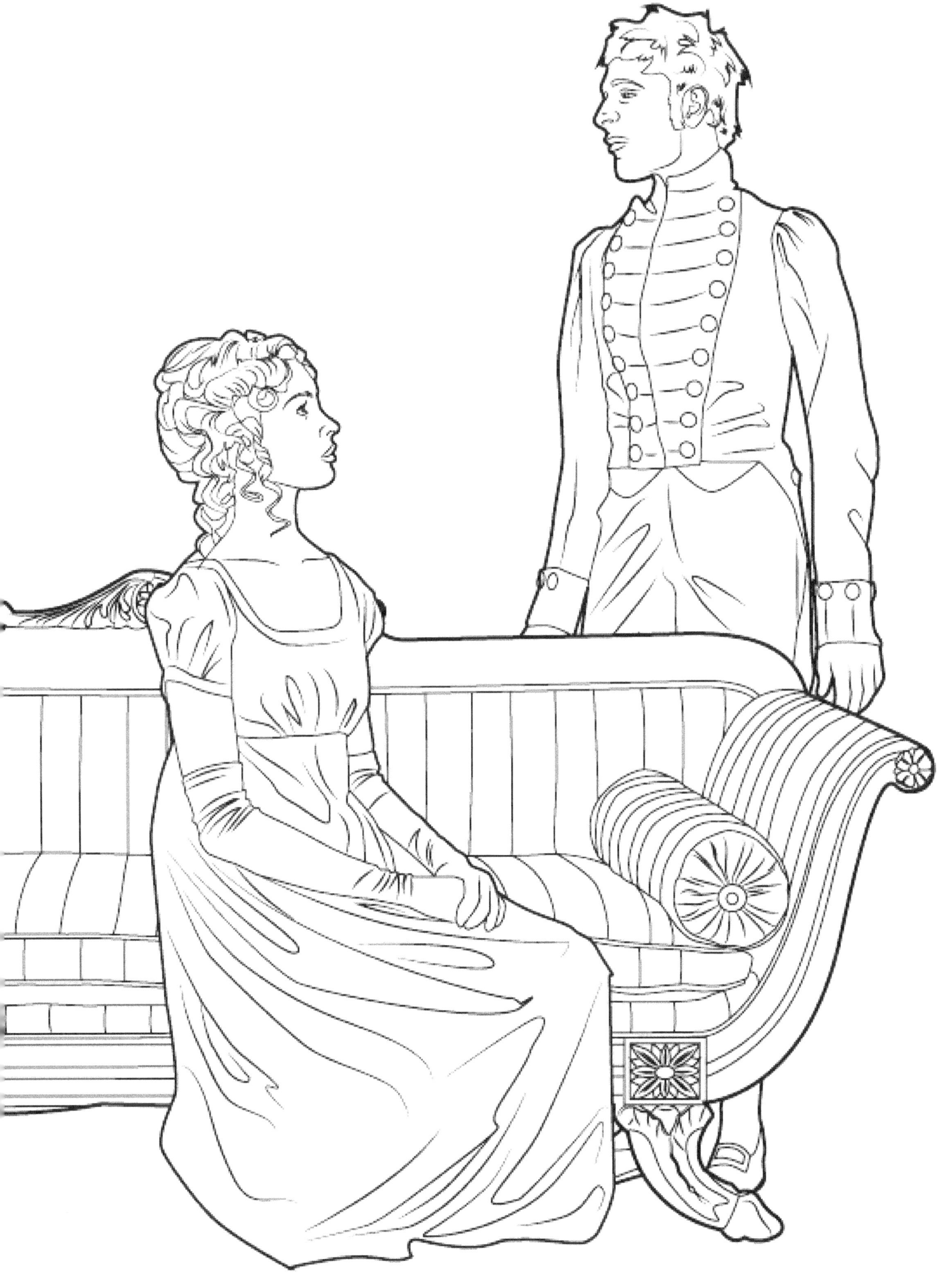

Other Coloring Books from Aryla Publishing

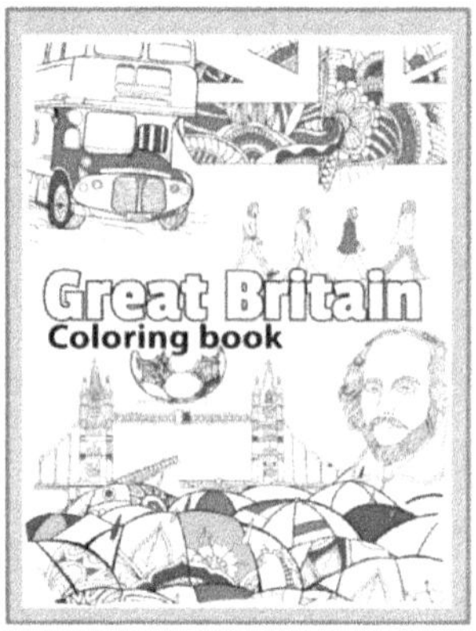

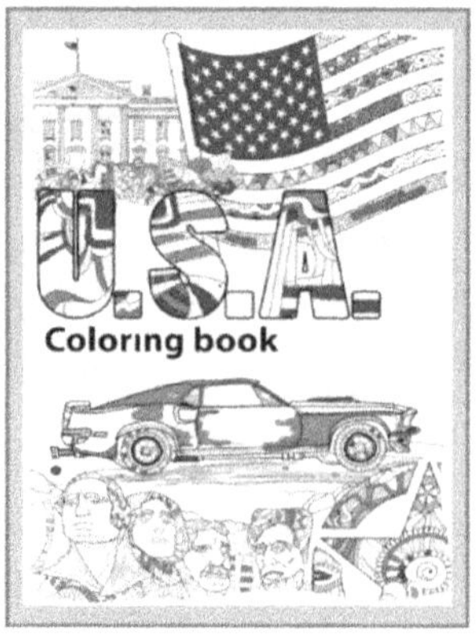

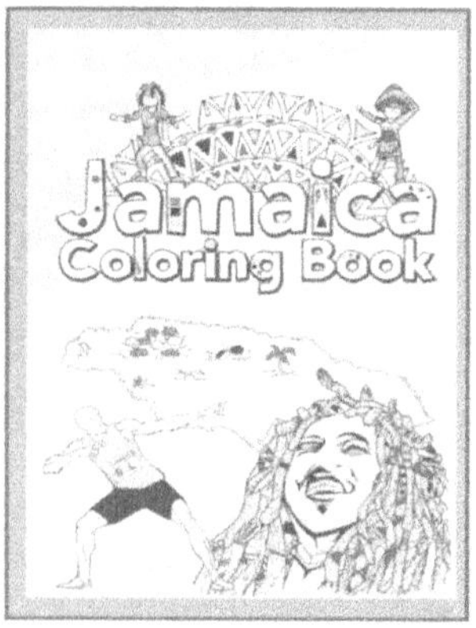

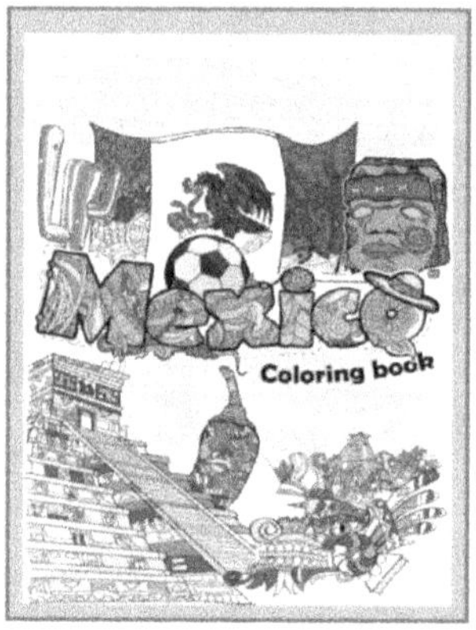

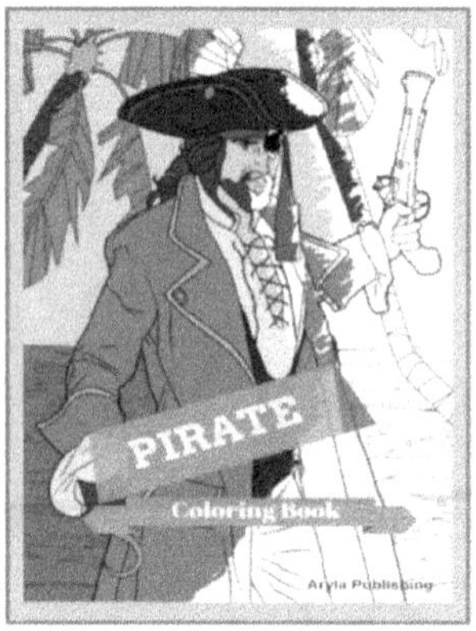

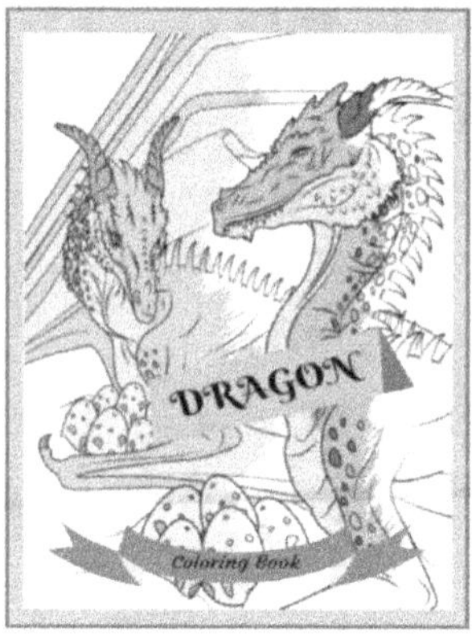

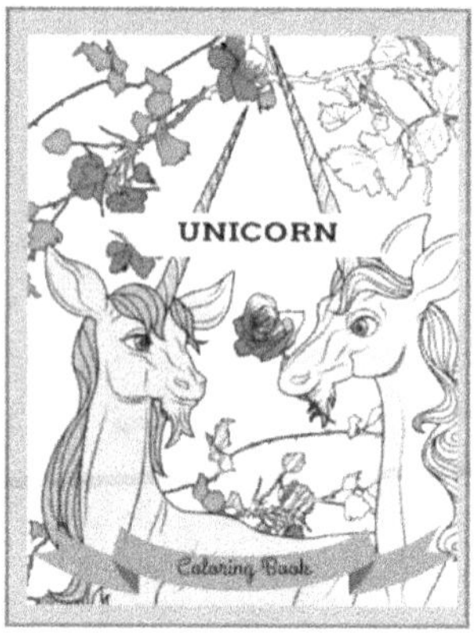

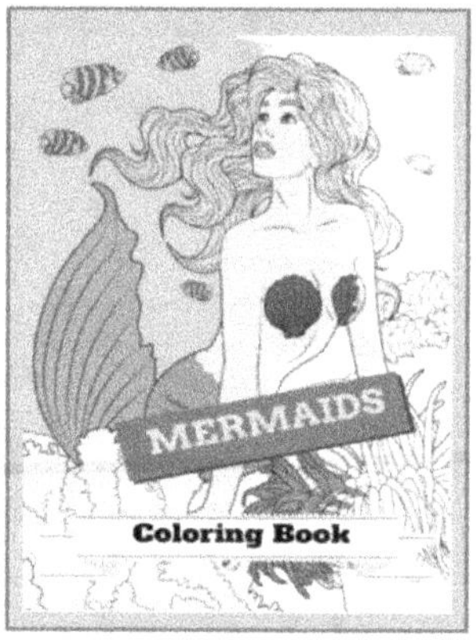

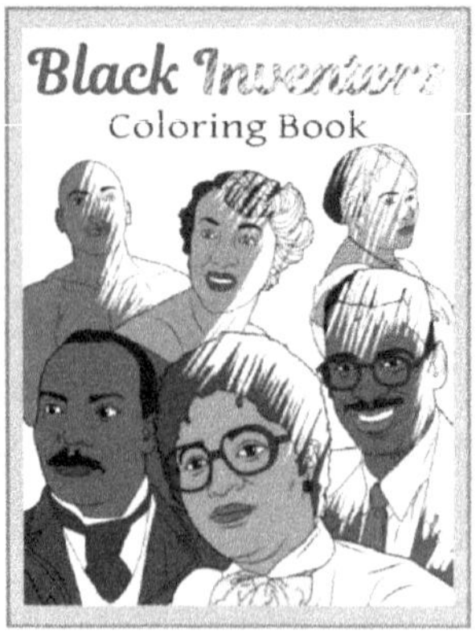

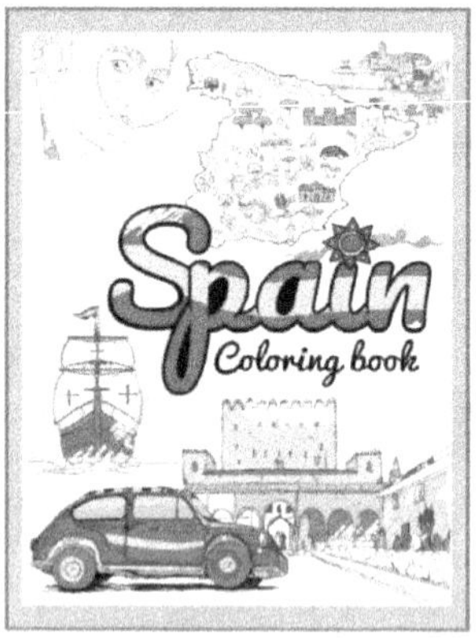

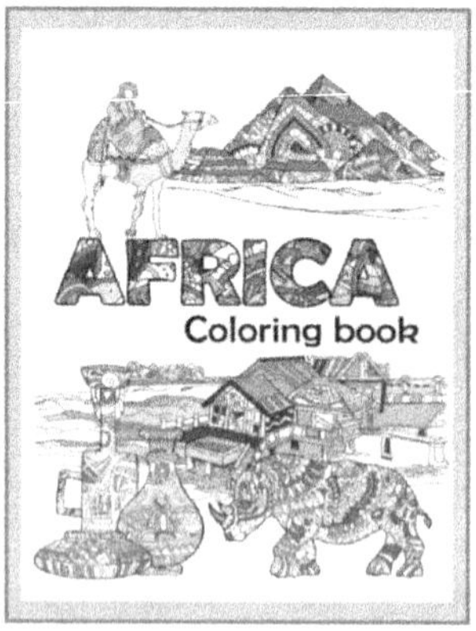

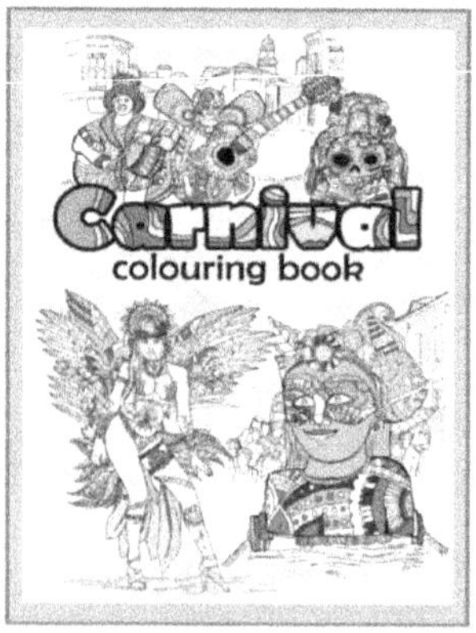

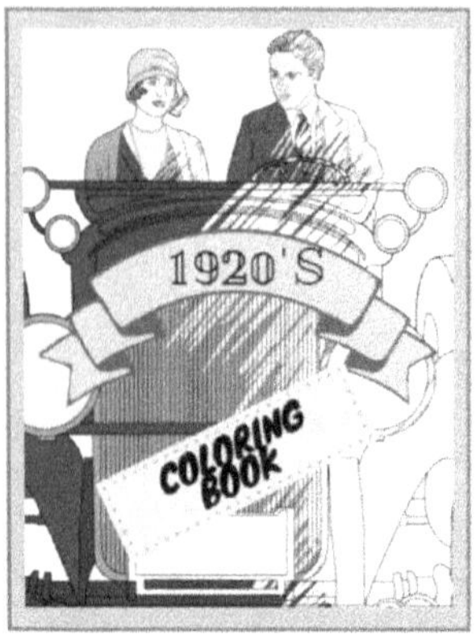

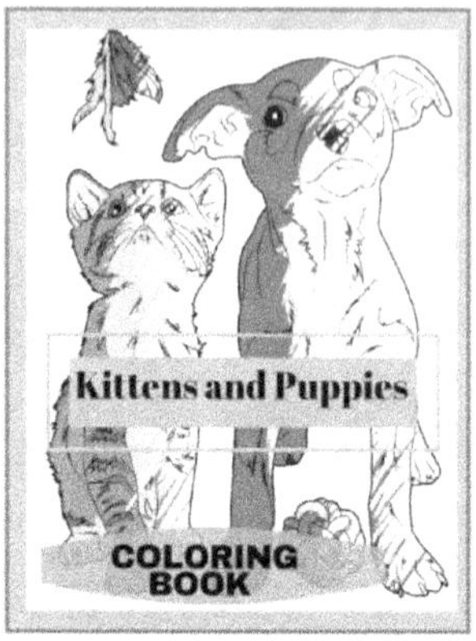

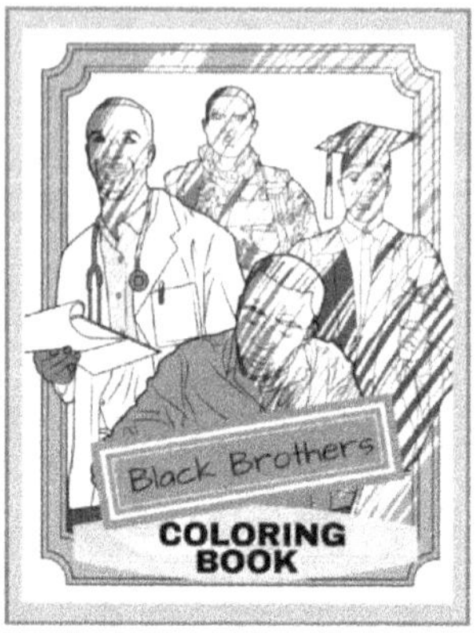

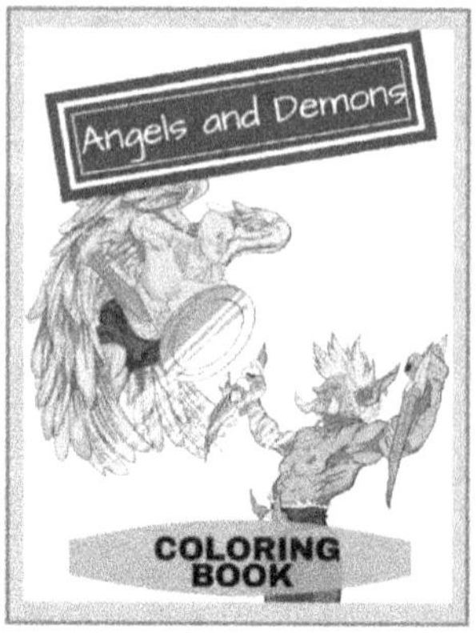

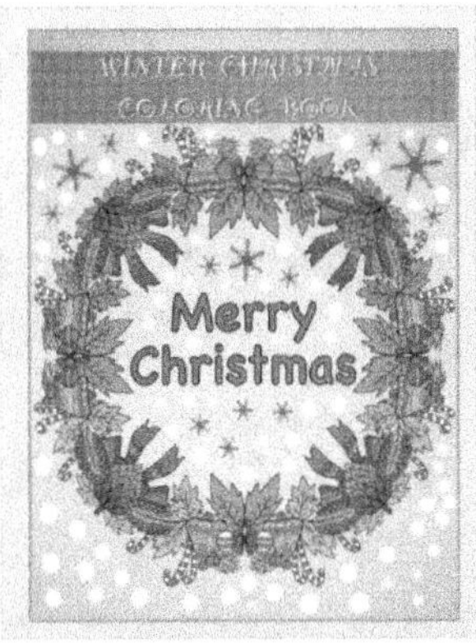
Merry Christmas
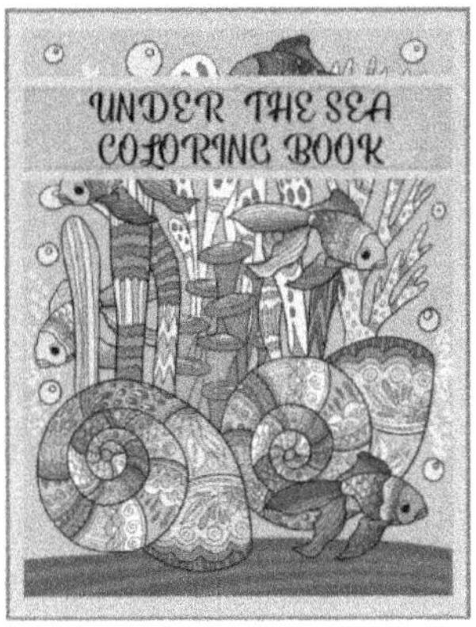
UNDER THE SEA
COLORING BOOK
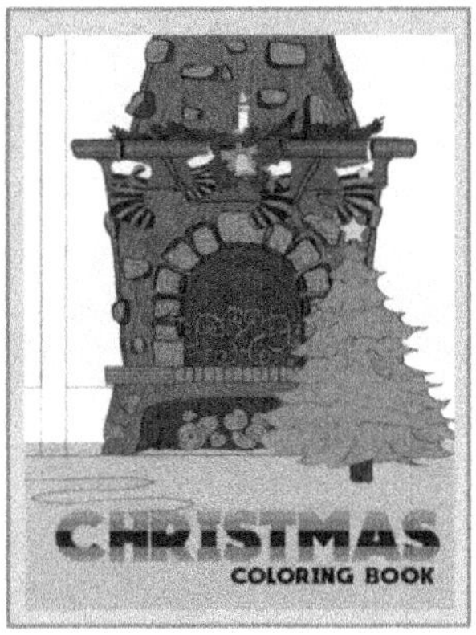
CHRISTMAS
COLORING BOOK
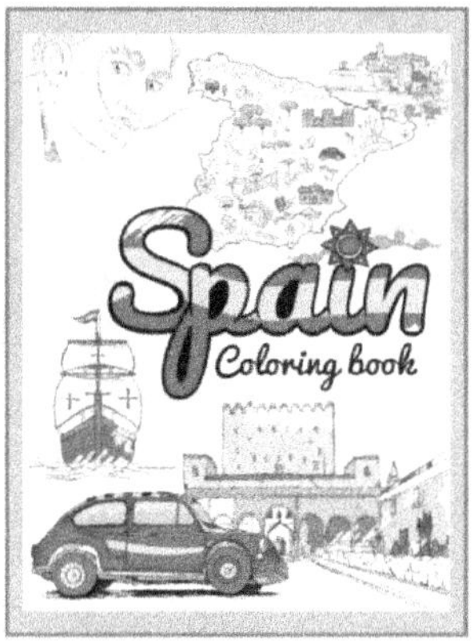
Spain
Coloring book
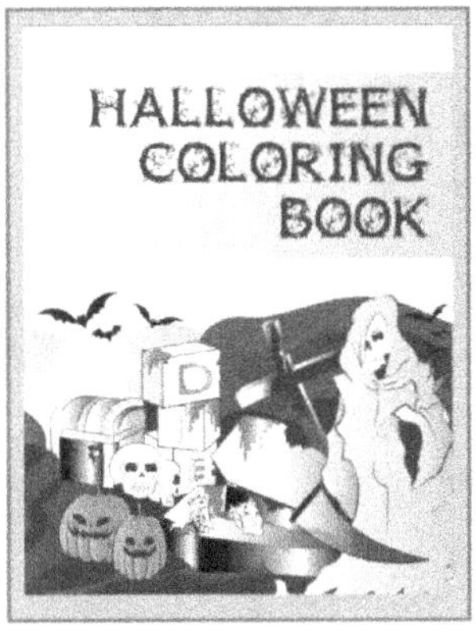
HALLOWEEN
COLORING
BOOK
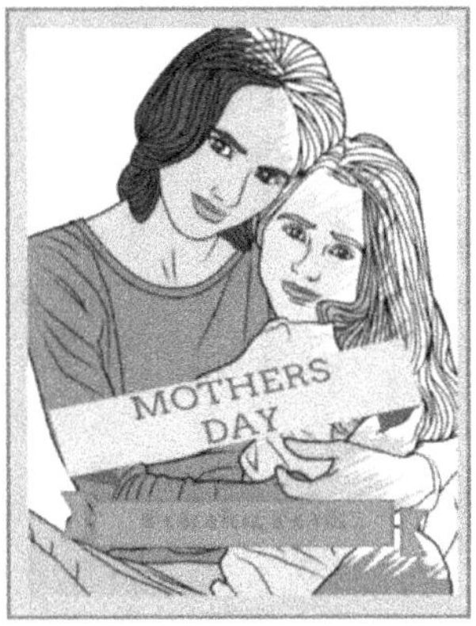
MOTHERS
DAY
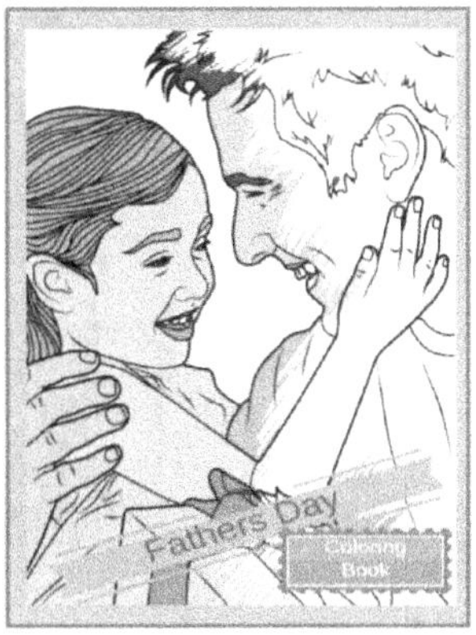
Fathers Day
Coloring
Book
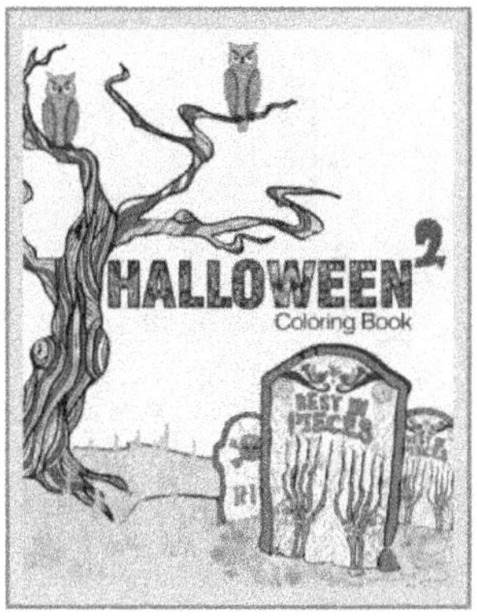
HALLOWEEN
Coloring Book
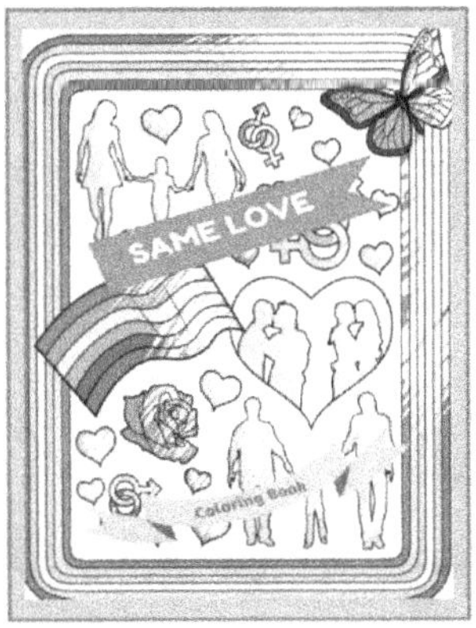
SAME LOVE
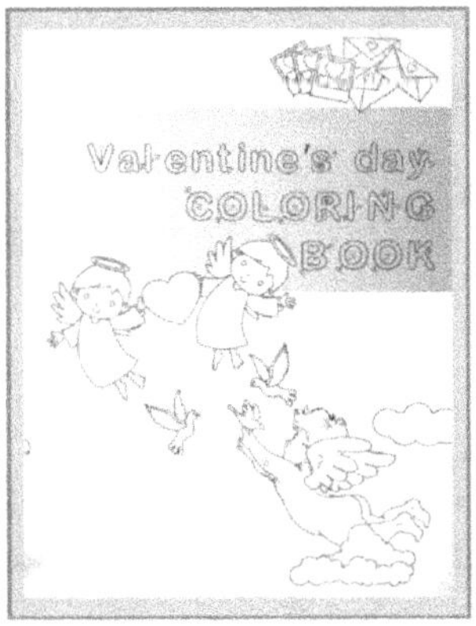
Valentine's day
COLORING
BOOK
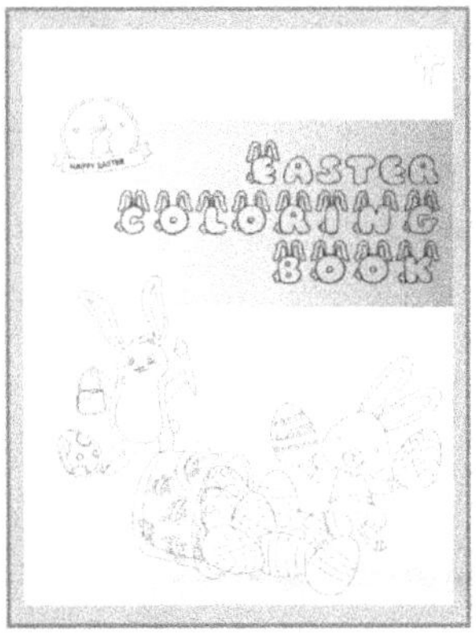
EASTER
COLORING
BOOK
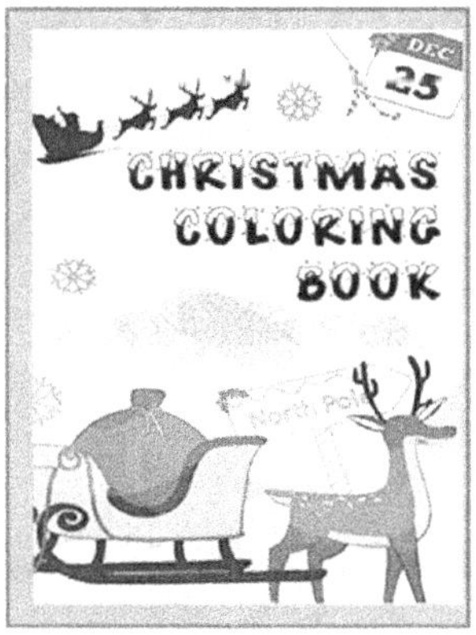
25
CHRISTMAS
COLORING
BOOK
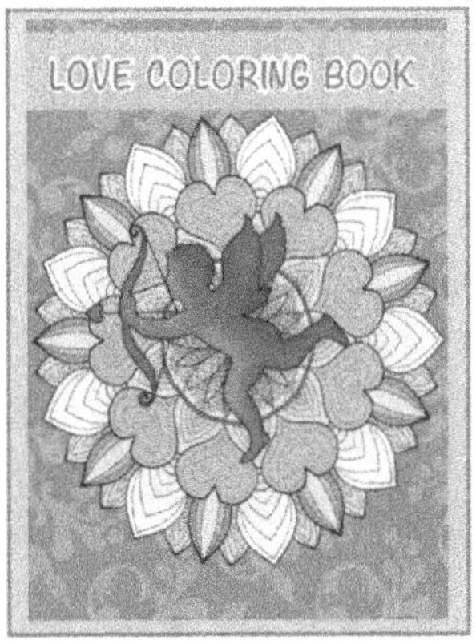
LOVE COLORING BOOK
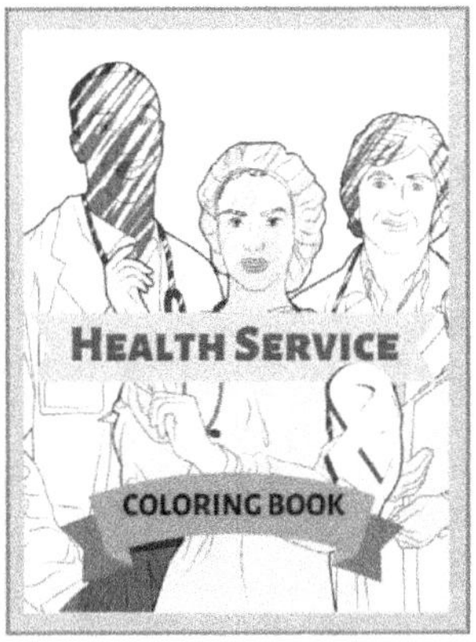
HEALTH SERVICE
COLORING BOOK
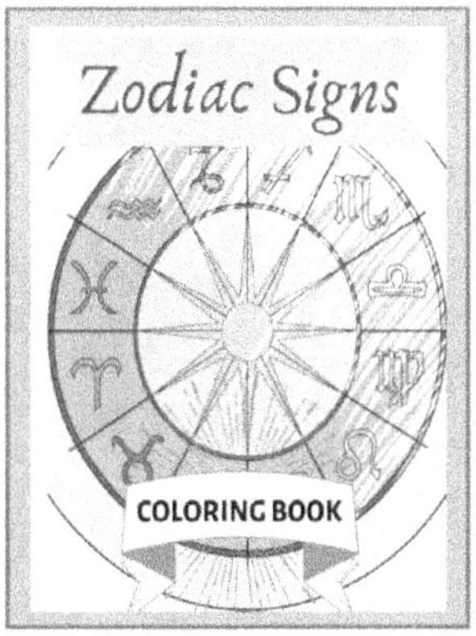
Zodiac Signs
COLORING BOOK
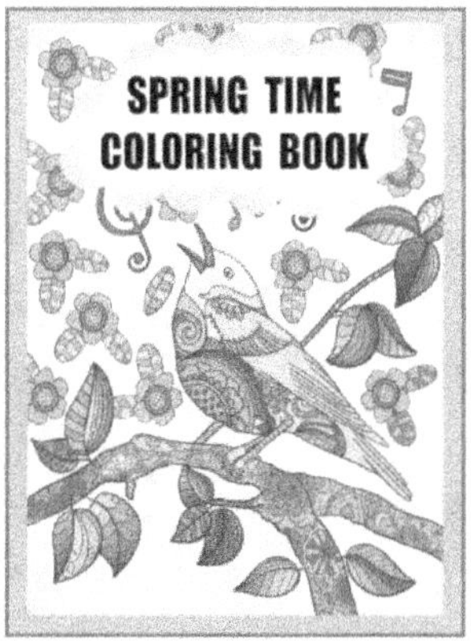
SPRING TIME
COLORING BOOK

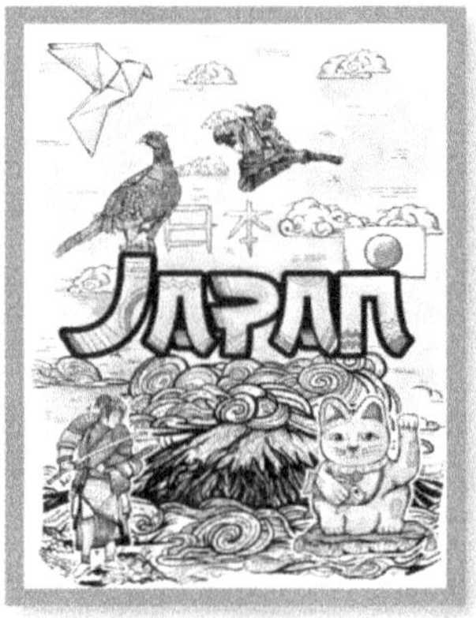
JAPAN

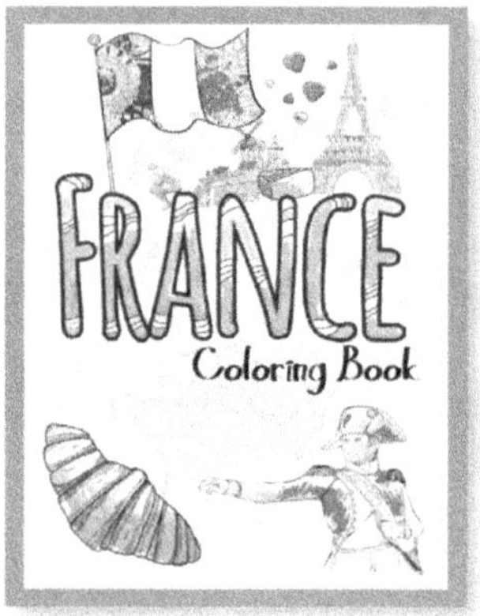
FRANCE
Coloring Book

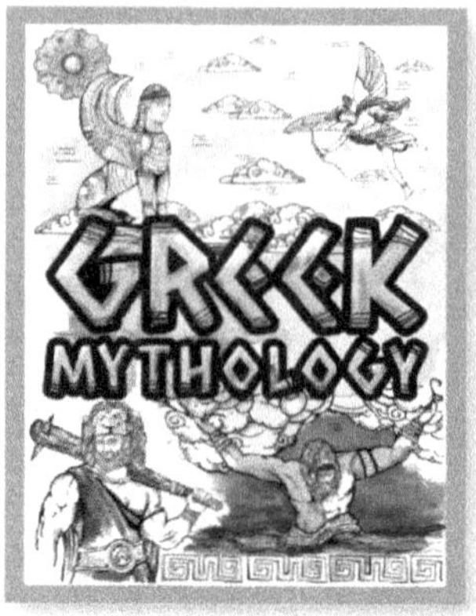
GREEK
MYTHOLOGY

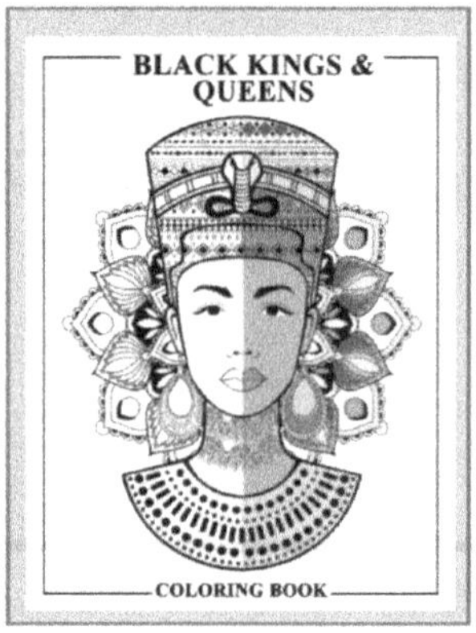
BLACK KINGS &
QUEENS
COLORING BOOK

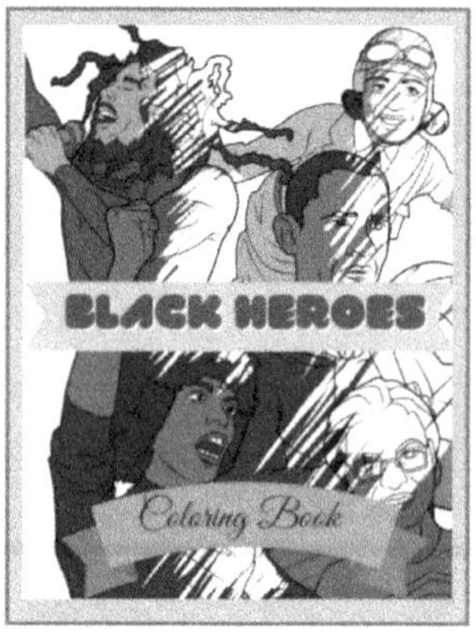
BLACK HEROES
Coloring Book

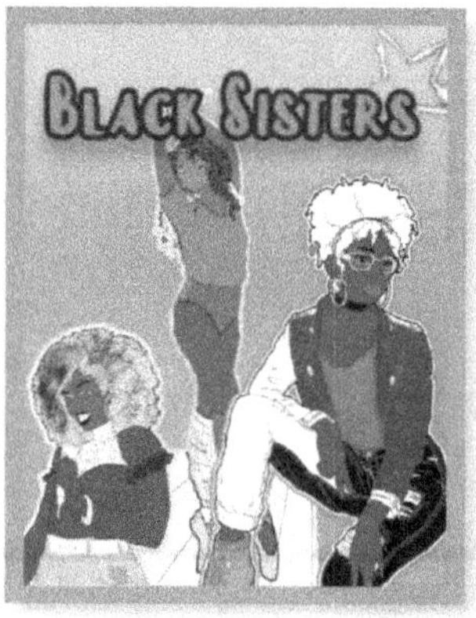
BLACK SISTERS

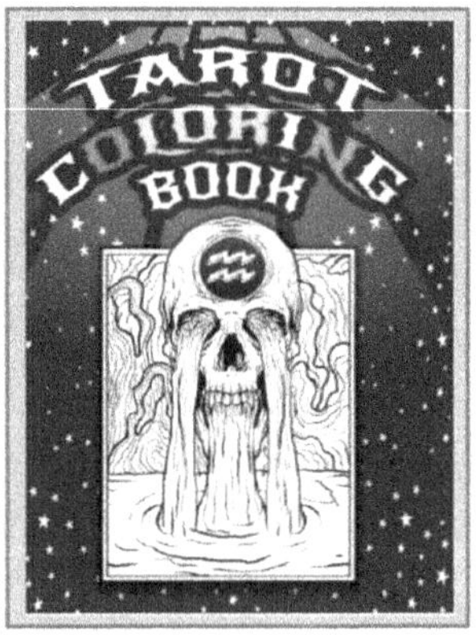
TAROT
COLORING
BOOK

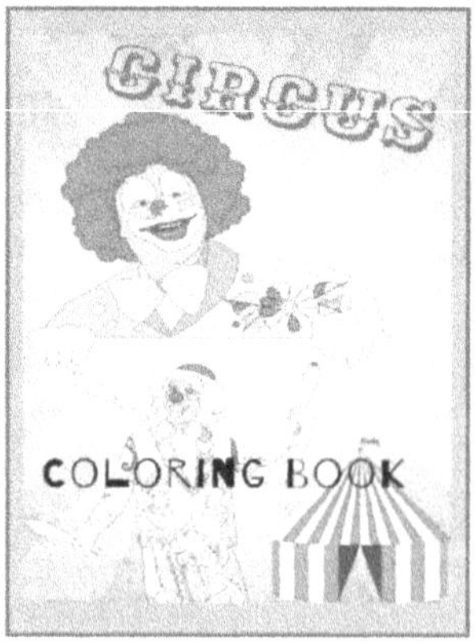
CIRCUS
COLORING BOOK

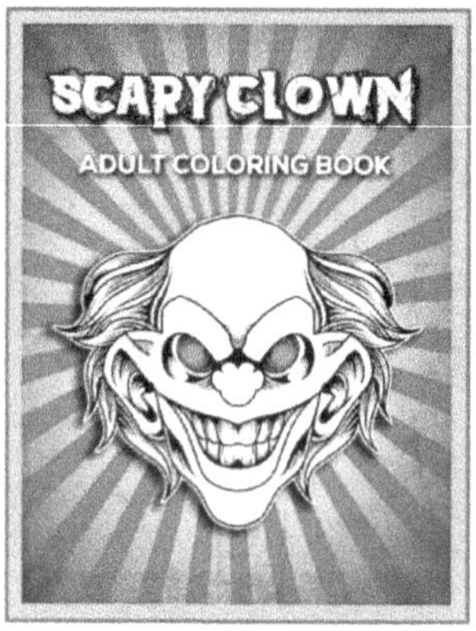
SCARY CLOWN
ADULT COLORING BOOK

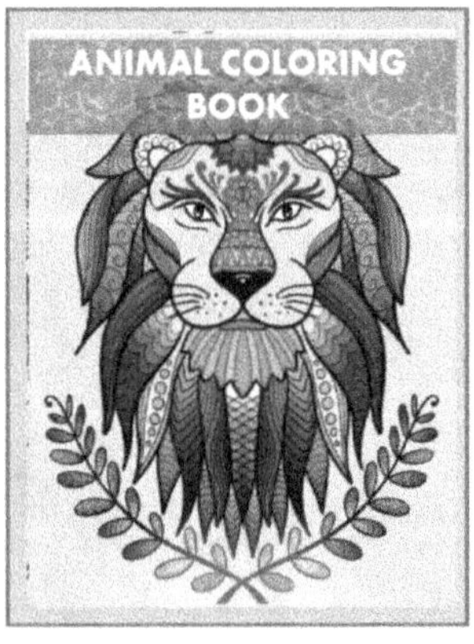
ANIMAL COLORING
BOOK

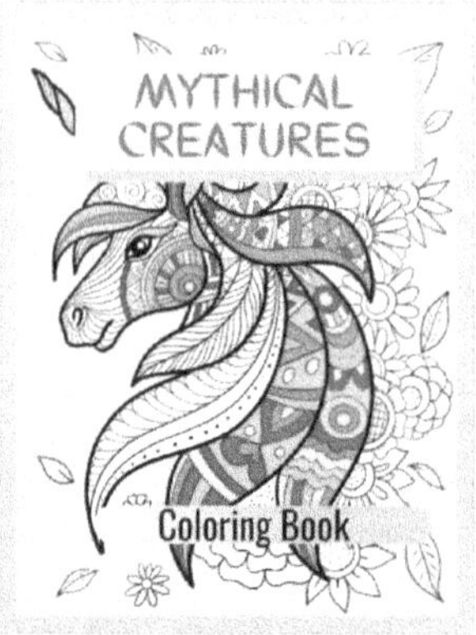
MYTHICAL
CREATURES
Coloring Book

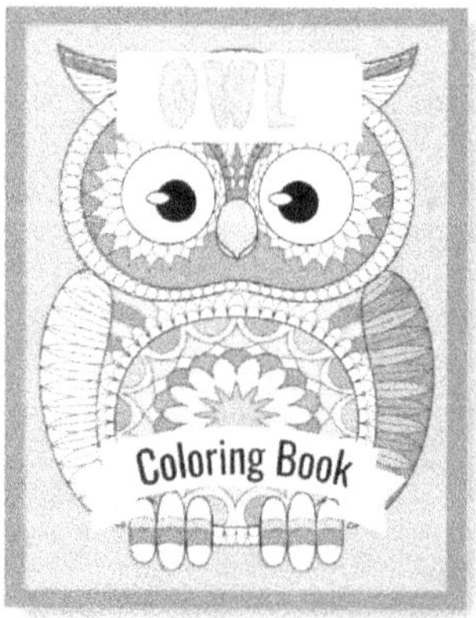
OWL
Coloring Book

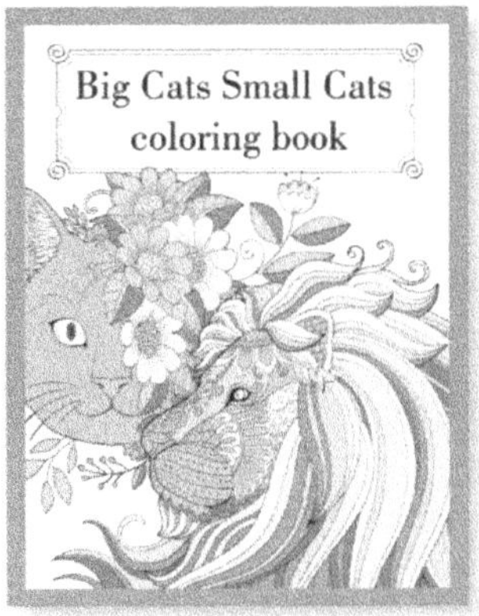
Big Cats Small Cats
coloring book

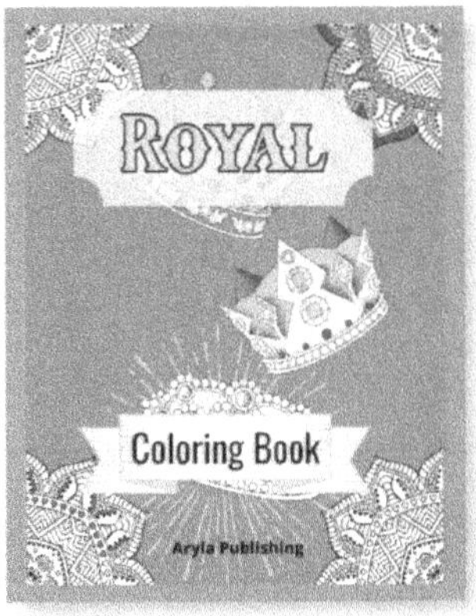
ROYAL
Coloring Book
Aryla Publishing

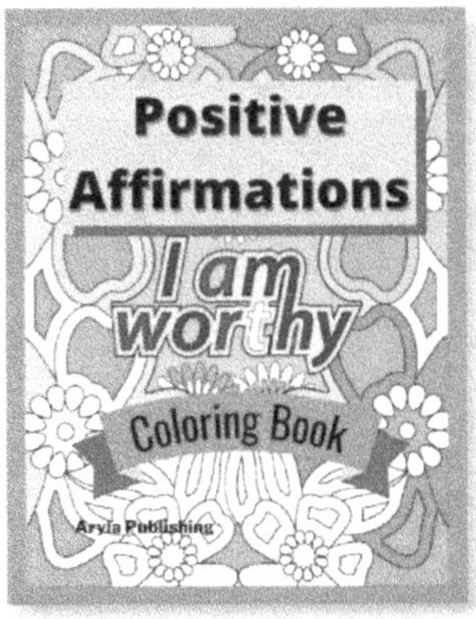
Positive
Affirmations
I am
worthy
Coloring Book
Aryla Publishing

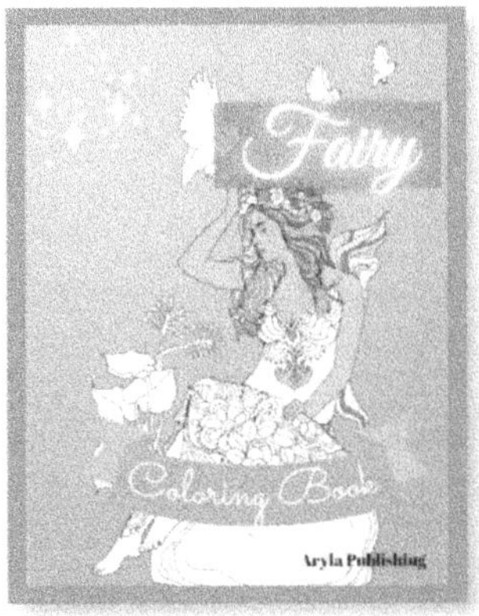
Fairy
Coloring Book
Aryla Publishing

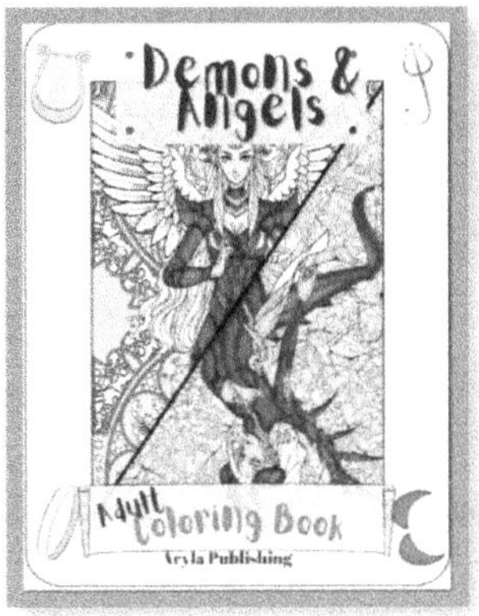
Demons &
Angels
Adult Coloring Book
Aryla Publishing

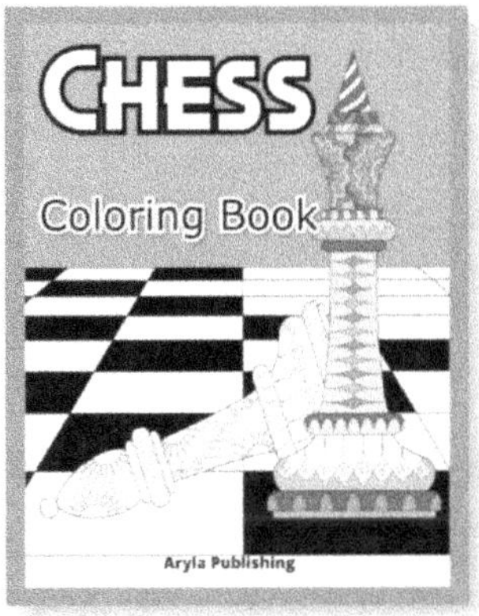
CHESS
Coloring Book
Aryla Publishing

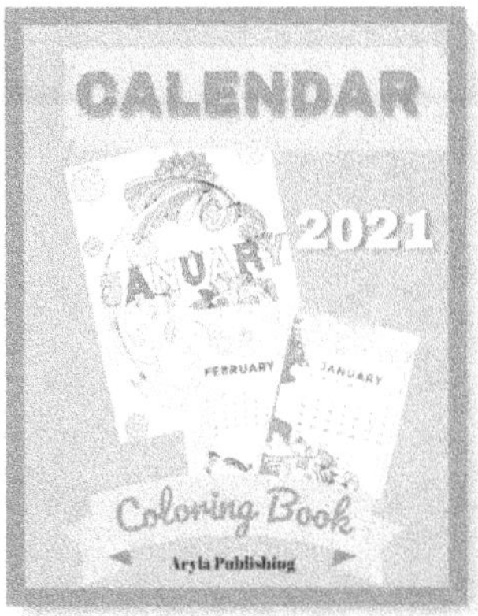
CALENDAR
2021
FEBRUARY
JANUARY
Coloring Book
Aryla Publishing

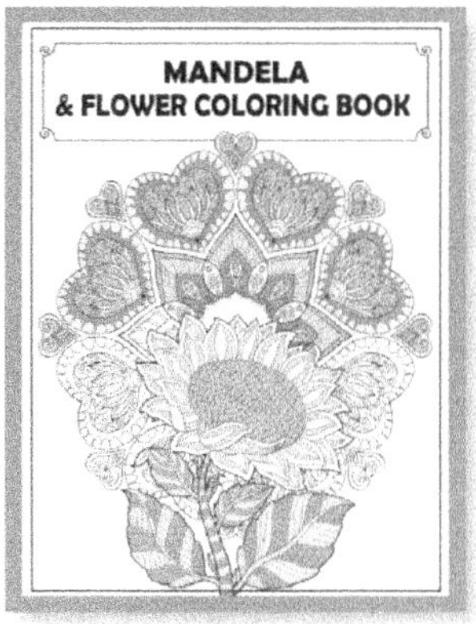
MANDELA
& FLOWER COLORING BOOK

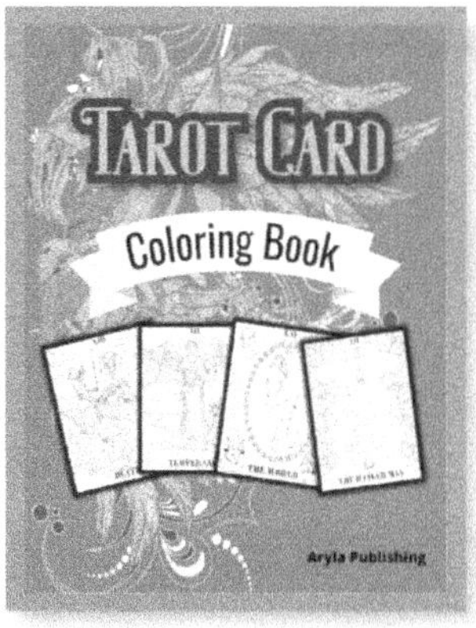
TAROT CARD
Coloring Book
Aryla Publishing

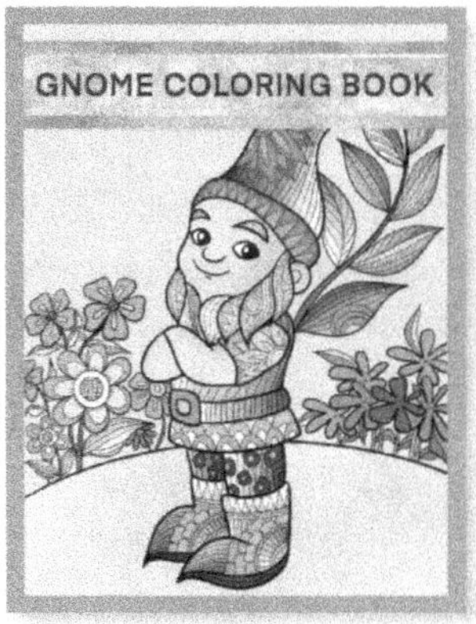
GNOME COLORING BOOK

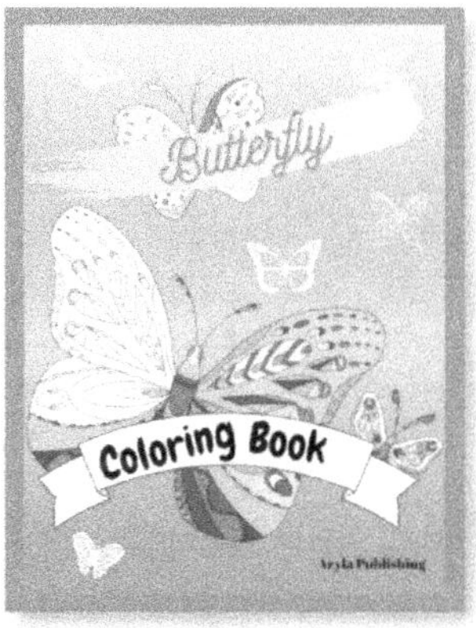
Butterfly
Coloring Book
Aryla Publishing

Color In Fun Kids Books

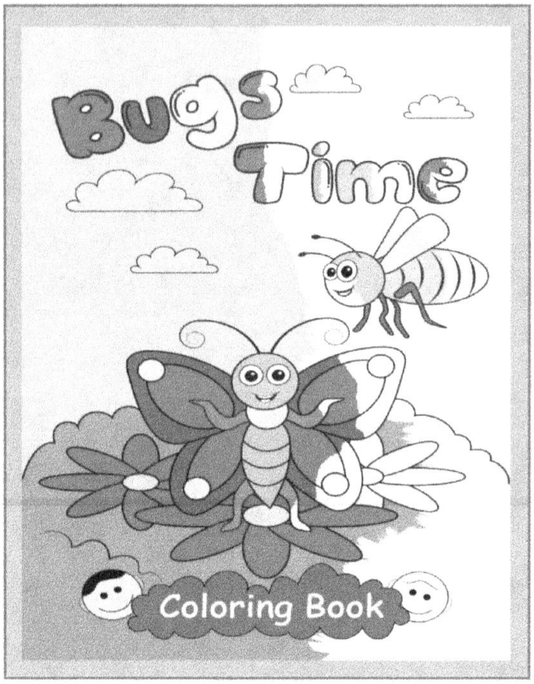

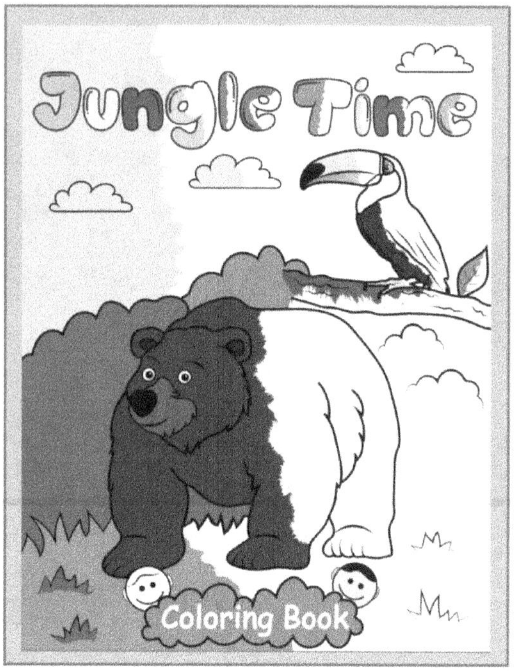

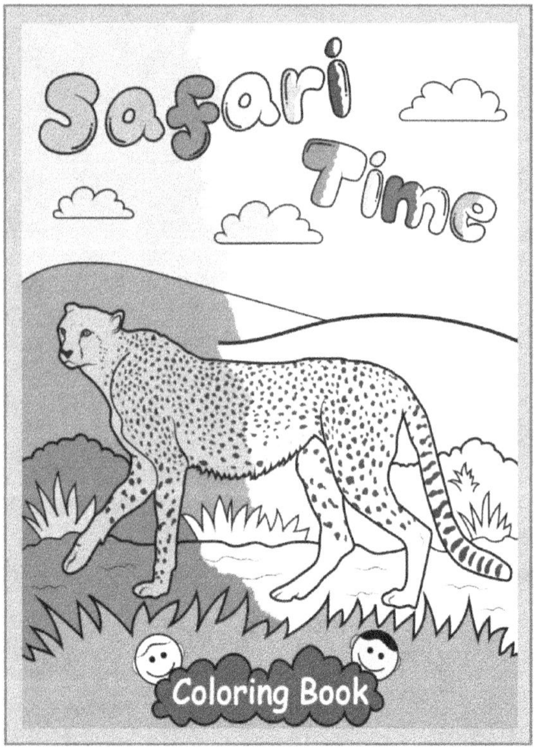

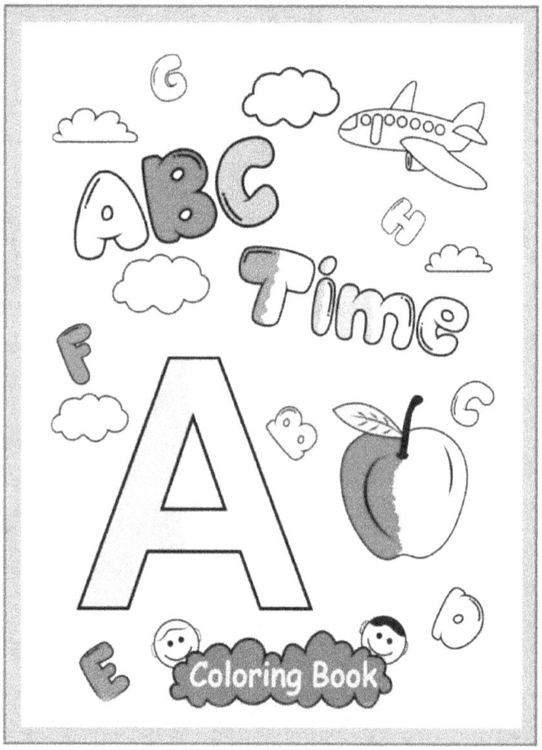

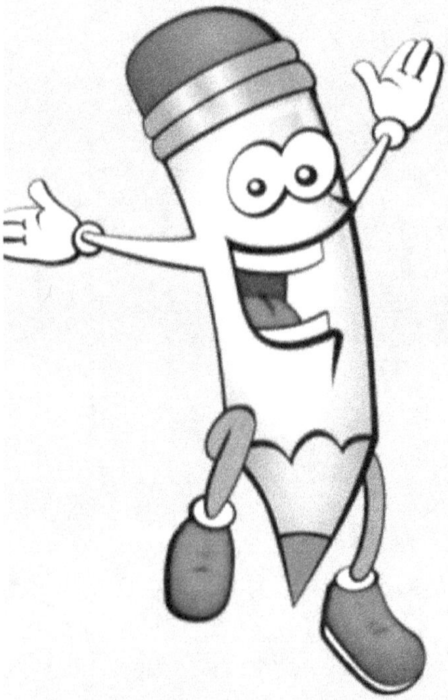

WE WOULD LOVE YOUR FEEDBACK

PLEASE LEAVE REVIEW AT:-

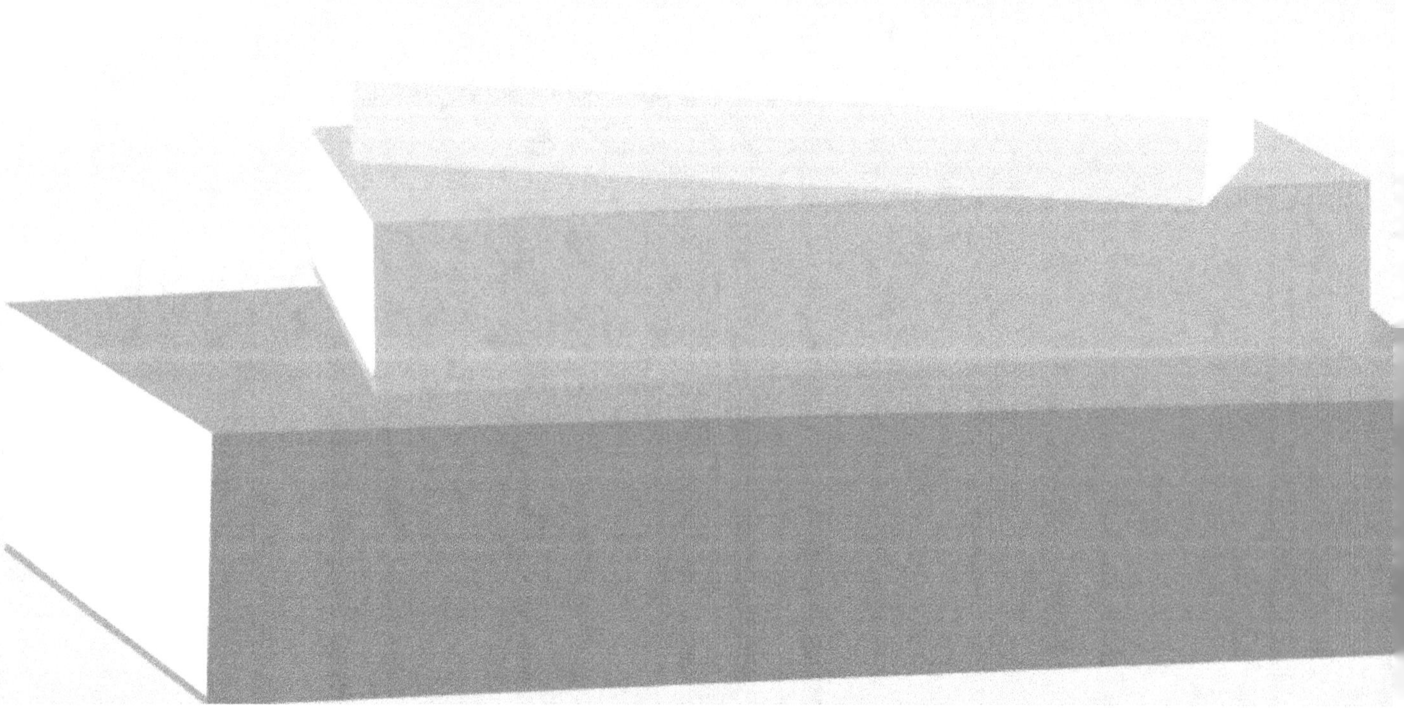

www.ingramcontent.com/pod-product-compliance
Lightning Source LLC
Chambersburg PA
CBHW080130240526
45468CB00009BA/2348
9781912675463